VIOLINJUDY'S
A VIOLIN TWINKLE
BOOK A

LEARN TO PLAY VIOLIN
METHOD BOOK WITH SONGS AND ACTIVITIES
FOR BEGINNING VIOLIN STUDENTS

Violin Judy's

VERY FUN VIOLIN COLLECTION

A Violin Twinkle Book A by Judy Naillon
Copyright ©2019 ViolinJudy
www.violinjudy.com
ISBN: 978-1-960674-04-3

Violin Judy's
VERY FUN VIOLIN LIBRARY

LEVEL A

A Violin Twinkle Book A is composed for violin students with no previous violin experience. Children using this book should be able to stand in the same spot for about 15 minutes while holding a foam or box violin to start or a real Violin. A book level chart for the *Very Fun Violin Collection* is provided at the end of this book.

HOW TO USE QR CODES IN THIS BOOK:

HOW TO SCAN A QR CODE WITH AN IPHONE OR IPAD:

IF YOU CAN TAKE A PICTURE YOU CAN SCAN A QR CODE!

SCAN ME

BOTH IPHONES AND IPADS HAVE A QR SCANNER BUILT INTO THE CAMERA.

1. WITH A QR CODE NEARBY, OPEN THE CAMERA ON YOUR IPHONE OR IPAD.

2. POSITION THE CAMERA SO THE QR CODE IS IN FRAME. YOUR IPHONE OR IPAD SHOULD SCAN IT AUTOMATICALLY, WITHOUT ANY INPUT NEEDED FROM YOU. ONCE IT SCANS THE CODE, A NOTIFICATION WILL APPEAR AT THE TOP OF YOUR SCREEN WITH THE LINK TO THE QR CODE'S CONTENT. TAP THIS AND YOU'LL BE BROUGHT TO IT.

HOW TO SCAN A QR CODE WITH AN ANDROID PHONE OR TABLET:

ANDROID DEVICES HAVE THE QR CODE SCANNER BUILT INTO THE CAMERA. HOWEVER, YOU MIGHT NEED TO OPEN A SPECIAL APP TO USE IT.

1. WITH A QR CODE NEARBY, OPEN THE CAMERA ON YOUR ANDROID DEVICE.

2. POSITION THE CAMERA SO THE QR CODE IS IN FRAME. YOUR ANDROID SHOULD SCAN IT AUTOMATICALLY, BUT IF IT DOESN'T, PRESS AND HOLD YOUR FINGER ON IT. YOU'LL BE GIVEN THE LINK THAT THE QR CODE LEADS TO AND A CHOICE TO OPEN IT, COPY THE URL, OR SHARE IT.
YOU CAN FIND ALL THESE LINKS ON MY KIDS' YOUTUBE PAGE, SEARCH #VIOLINJUDY

SET UP YOUR VIOLIN WITH FINGERING TAPES:

Full Size Violin (4/4)
Tape 1 – 35mm (1 3/8 inches)
Tape 2 – 66mm (2 5/8 inches)
Tape 3 – 80mm (3 1/8 inches)
Tape 4 – 106mm (4 1/8 inches)

3/4 Violin
Tape 1 – 32mm (1 1/4 inches)
Tape 2 – 61mm (2 3/8 inches)
Tape 3 – 75 mm (2 7/8 inches)
Tape 4 – 100 mm (3 7/8 inches)

1/2 Violin
Tape 1 – 28mm (1 1/8 inches)
Tape 2 – 54mm (2 1/8 inches)
Tape 3 – 68mm (2 5/8 inches)
Tape 4 – 91mm (3 5/8 inches)

1/4 Violin
Tape 1 – 25mm (1 inch)
Tape 2 – 48mm (1 7/8 inches)
Tape 3 – 60mm (2 3/8 inches)
Tape 4 – 79mm (3 1/8 inches)

You can put a finger tape on your Violin for every finger but you only need two tapes- one for finger #1 in the natural position and one for finger #3. Finger two ALWAYS snuggles up next to finger three in this book. The above chart will help you determine where to place each tape on your specific size violin!
Measure from below the nut -see the above arrow for where to start.

WHERE TO GET A VIOLIN?

Any major city will have a luthier shop-a luthier is a person who specializes in making, repairing and selling stringed instruments. You can rent or purchase a Violin. If you do not have a luthier near you, SharMusic.com is an excellent resource for an affordable student Violin.   Please avoid buying what we violin teachers call "Violin Shaped Objects" or VSO's from Ebay and Amazon. Every year I have student who are so excited to begin learning but have a poor quality instrument that won't stay in tune. This is very frustrating as the student, practice helper or teacher will spend a lot of time just trying to get the instrument to stay in tune. A good way to tell if you have a real violin or VSO is to look at the (see the arrow below) "nut" -it should be about the width of a business card higher than the fingerboard, lifting the strings slightly off the fingerboard. Remember that those five star glowing reviews on Amazon can be purchased, and you get what you pay for!

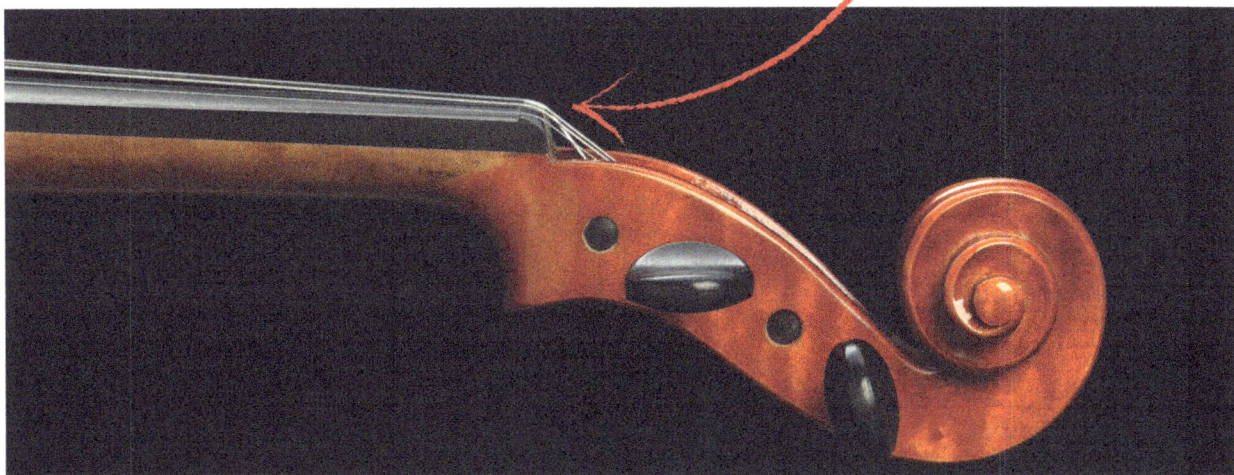

NOTE TO TEACHERS/PRACTICE PARENT:

Any Violin Student with some experience correctly holding and playing the open strings of the Violin can start in this book on a real instrument. For a total beginner *A Violin Twinkle A* will be a more helpful book to start! The pacing of this series is slower than any other method book you will find. This allows younger beginners time to play a wide variety of songs and establish a firm foundation of technic, listening skills while having FUN. Playing pieces that are traditional and familiar, yet presented in a fun, fresh way engages the learner.

We start with floating off-the-staff notes as well as notes on the staff (real music). The pacing is graded in a manner that the note reading will not be overwhelming and the note names are placed inside the noteheads as an aide and phase out towards the end of the book. Having a printed paper with links to practice reminder videos to send home with children helps parents remember what to do, and children are often able to practice these without help after the first few lessons. You may use this book as a pre-cursor to method books like Suzuki Violin Book 1 or in conjunction. I treat the last half of this book like Etudes.

In this book you will find many
tools to help your students learn the Violin including
-diagrams
-worksheets
-science of music pages
These songs are fun to play in group lessons as well!
Students who have successfully completed this book can look forward to
A Violin Twinkle Book Level B and *Level C,*
A Violin Fall, Halloween, Winter & Christmas Books!

CARING FOR YOUR VIOLIN:

TREAT YOUR VIOLIN LIKE A SMALL BABY. VIOLINS ARE NOT INDESTRUCTIBLE. THEY ARE HELD TOGETHER WITH WOOD GLUE WHICH CAN EASILY BECOME UN-GLUED IF YOU LEAVE YOUR INSTRUMENT IN HOT/COLD/HUMID/DRY CONDITIONS. IF YOU NEED TO GO TO THE GROCERY STORE BEFORE OR AFTER YOUR LESSON, YOU MUST ALSO TAKE YOUR VIOLIN IN THE STORE! AFTER ALL, YOU WOULD NOT LEAVE YOUR BABY IN THE CAR! MOST CASES COME WITH BACKPACK STRAPS OR A PLACE WHERE BACKPACK STRAPS CAN BE ADDED.

KEEP YOUR VIOLIN IN YOUR HOME IN A SAFE PLACE, AWAY FROM PETS OR YOUNGER CURIOUS SIBLINGS. A SPECIAL WALL HANGER CALLED A "STRING SWING" IS AVAILABLE FROM AMAZON OR SHAR MUSIC AND IS A GREAT WAY TO DISPLAY YOUR INSTRUMENT AND IS A VISUAL REMINDER TO PRACTICE!

BE SURE TO CAREFULLY WIPE YOUR VIOLIN OFF OF ROSIN AND FINGERPRINTS WITH A CLEAN, DRY COTTON CLOTH AFTER EACH TIME YOU PRACTICE AND WIPE THE STICK OF THE BOW VERY CAREFULLY EACH WEEK. ALWAYS REMEMBER TO REMOVE YOUR SHOULDER REST FROM YOUR INSTRUMENT BEFORE PLACING IT BACK IN THE CASE.

IN THE WINTER WHEN YOUR SKIN GETS DRY AND YOU NEED LOTION, YOUR VIOLIN FEELS THE SAME WAY! INSTEAD OF LOTION, YOUR VIOLIN NEEDS HUMIDITY. YOU CAN PLACE A COOL MIST HUMIDIFIER IN THE ROOM WHERE YOUR VIOLIN LIVES, OR PURCHASE A SPECIAL HUMIDIFIER CALLED A "DAMP-IT" (NICKNAMED A GREEN SNAKE) WHICH YOU NEED TO FILL WITH WATER DAILY, SQUEEZE THE EXCESS OUT, DRY THE GREEN TUBE AND INSERT CAREFULLY INTO THE F HOLE ON THE SIDE OPPOSITE YOUR SOUND POST. YOU CAN PURCHASE A "DAMP-IT" FROM SHAR MUSIC OR AMAZON. ANOTHER POPULAR TYPE OF HUMIDIFIER FOR YOUR VIOLIN IS A SPECIAL SILICONE POUCH, HOWEVER THESE PACKETS NEED TO BE REPLACED WHEN THEY BECOME ROCK HARD.

STUDENTS WITH FOAM OR BOX VIOLINS SHOULD ALSO TAKE SPECIAL CARE OF THEIR INSTRUMENT TO GET INTO THE HABIT OF TREATING THE VIOLIN WELL!

YOU CAN FIND A LIST OF HUMIDIFIERS AT VIOLINJUDY.COM

WAKING UP YOUR VIOLIN & BOW:

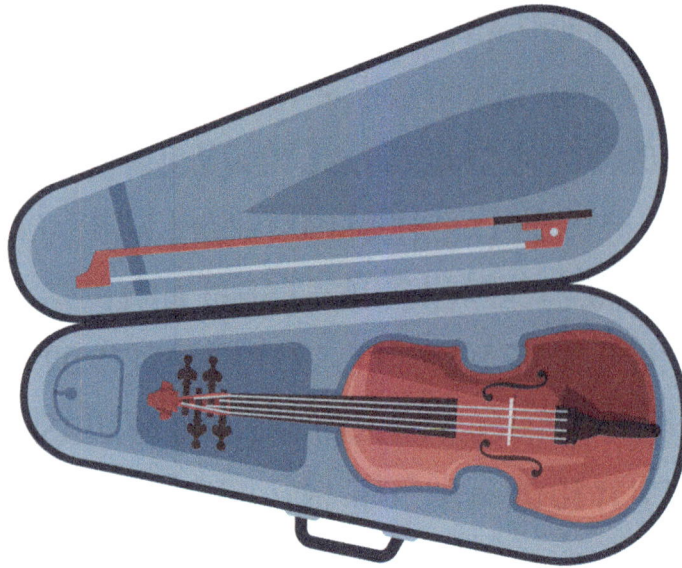

-WASH AND DRY YOUR HANDS!

-PLACE YOUR MUSIC ON THE STAND

-OPEN YOUR CASE

-TAKE OUT YOUR BOW

-TIGHTEN YOUR BOW BY TURNING IT ABOUT EIGHT TIMES(REMEMBER "RIGHTY TIGHTY-LEFTY LOOSEY")

-PUT THREE SWIPES OF ROSIN UP AND DOWN YOUR BOW

-PUT YOUR BOW ON THE MUSIC STAND

-PUT ON YOUR SHOULDER REST (SEE NEXT PAGE)

-PUT YOUR VIOLIN UNDER YOUR RIGHT (BOW) ARM

PUTTING ON YOUR SHOULDER REST:

WHEN YOU BEGIN TO PLAY VIOLIN YOU MAY USE A CLEAN, DRY, KITCHEN SPONGE (WITH NO ABRASIVE SURFACE) AND A RUBBER BAND TO ATTACH IT TO YOUR VIOLIN. YOU CAN USE THE PICTURES BELOW TO HELP YOU PUT ON YOUR SHOULDER REST.

AFTER A FEW WEEKS YOU WILL WANT YOU TO USE A SHOULDER REST. SOME POPULAR BRANDS ARE KUN, WOLF, OR EVEREST. YOU CAN FIND ALL OF THESE AND MORE AT SHAR MUSIC. YOU MAY NEED TO TRY SOME DIFFERENT SHOULDER RESTS TO FIND THE PERFECT FIT FOR BOTH YOUR VIOLIN AND YOUR SHOULDER! THE SIDE CLOSEST TO YOUR BELLY BUTTON SHOULD BE TALL AND THE SIDE NEAR YOUR SHOULDER (AND NEAR YOUR CHIN REST) WILL BE SHORTER.

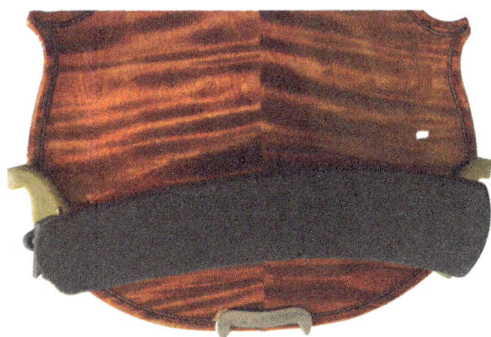

GOOD MANNERS OF VIOLIN: A TRADITION

-WHEN WE ARE READY TO START OUR LESSON WE PUT OUR VIOLIN IN "REST POSITION" (SEE P. 10) TAKE A BOW AND SAY "I AM READY TO LEARN."

-WHEN WE ARE DONE WITH THE VIOLIN LESSON WE PUT OUR VIOLIN IN "REST POSITION" TAKE ANOTHER BOW AND SAY "THANK YOU FOR TEACHING ME! "

AT HOME YOU CAN DO THE SAME THING, SAYING "THANK YOU FOR HELPING ME LEARN" TO YOUR PARENT OR PRACTICE PARTNER!

-YOU MAY LIKE TO CUT OUT THE NEXT PAGE OF YOUR BOOK AND LEAVE IT ON YOUR STAND FOR A "GOOD MANNERS" REMINDER!

String Family

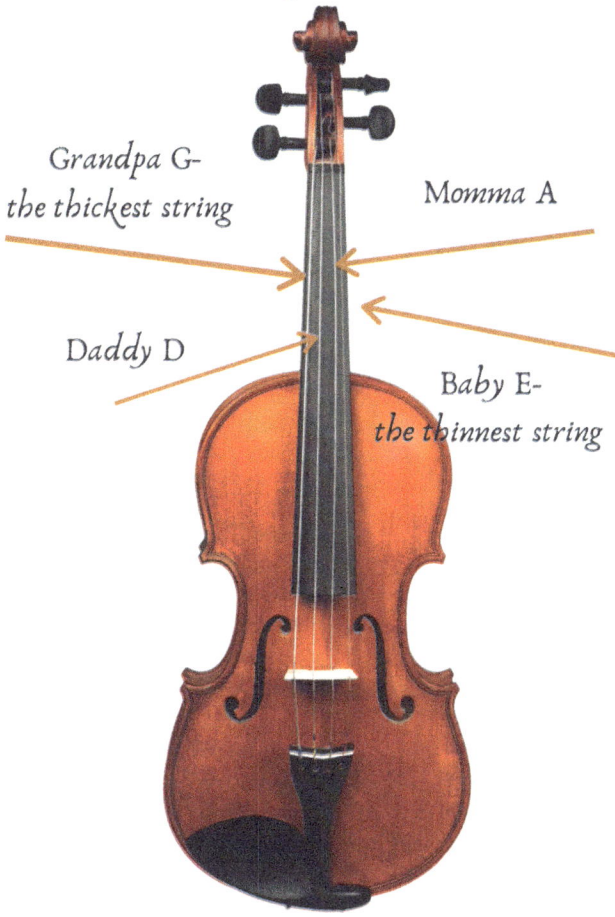

Grandpa G–
the thickest string

Momma A

Daddy D

Baby E–
the thinnest string

Basic Parts of the Bow

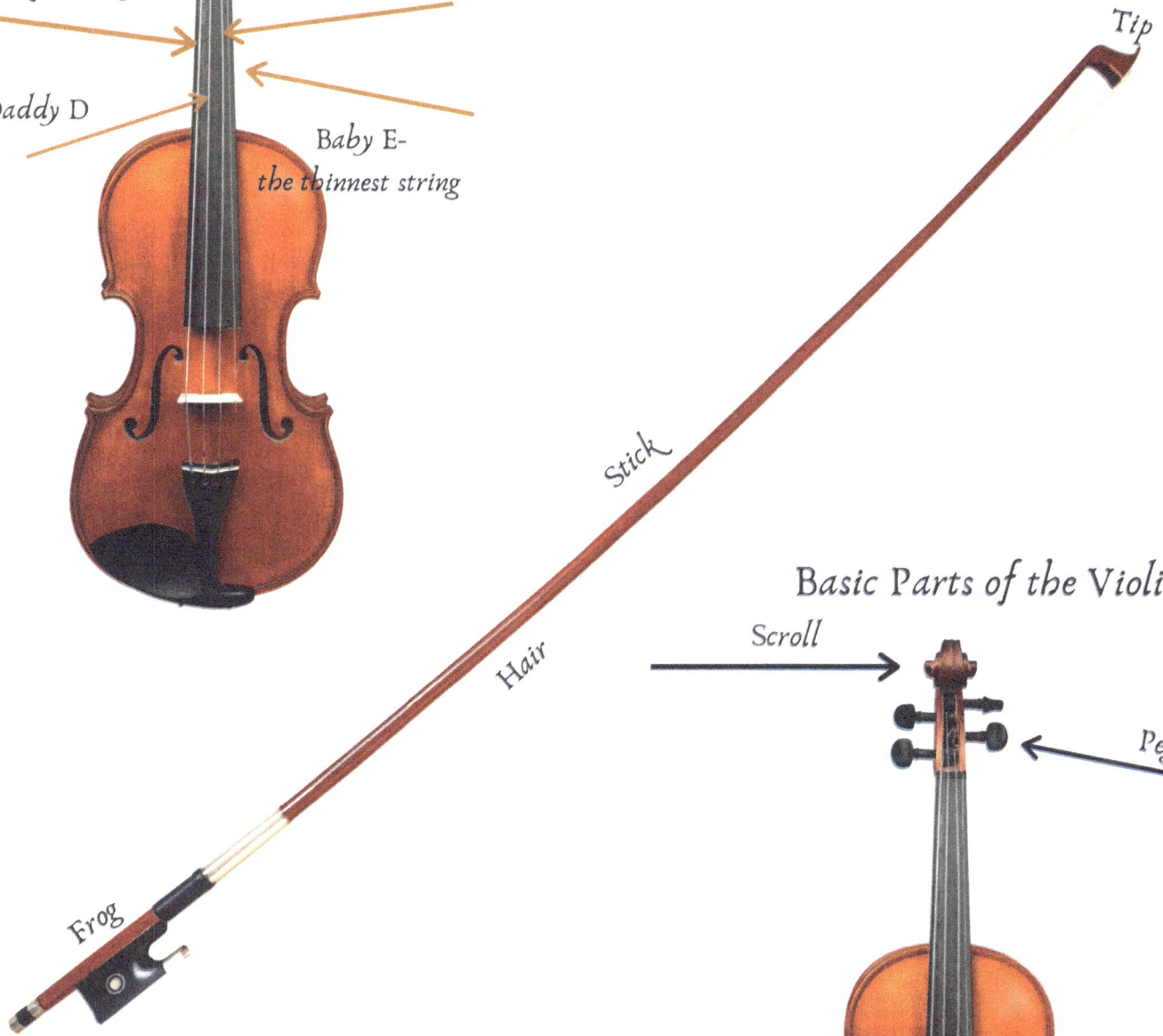

Tip

Stick

Hair

Frog

Basic Parts of the Violin

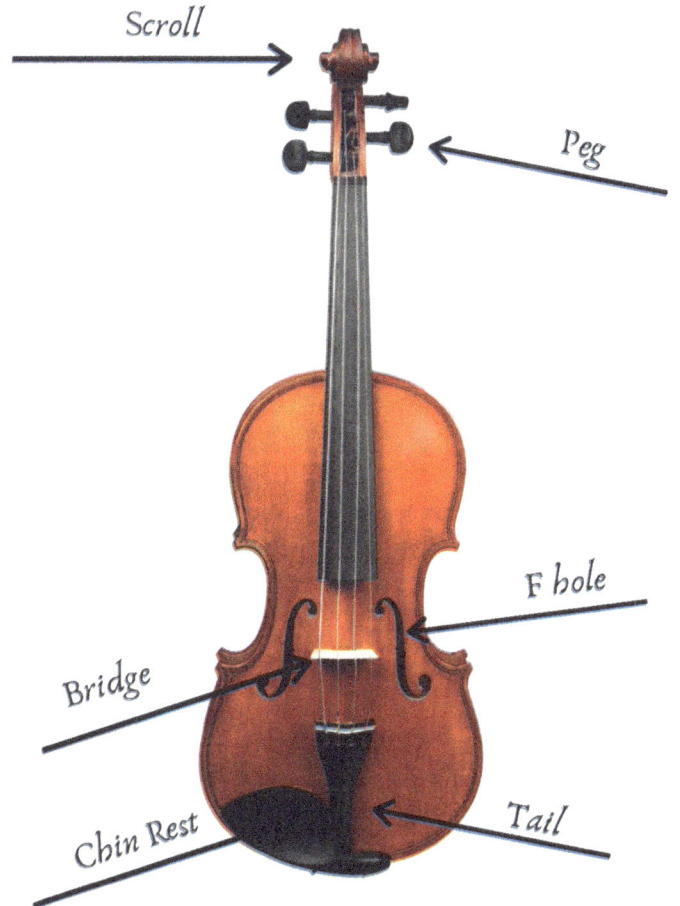

Scroll

Peg

F hole

Bridge

Chin Rest

Tail

SCAN ME

PUTTING VIOLIN & BOW AWAY:

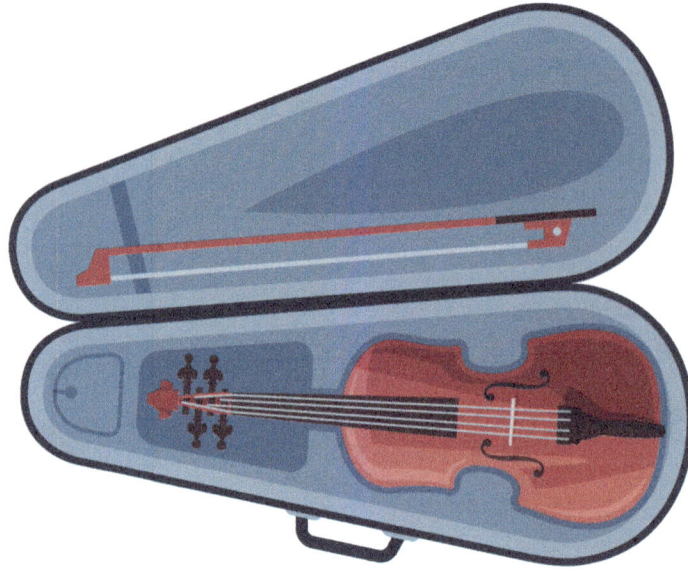

- LOOSEN YOUR BOW 8 TIMES
- PUT YOUR BOW BACK IN THE CASE
- REMOVE YOUR SHOULDER REST FROM VIOLIN
- RETURN SHOULDER REST TO IT'S HOME
- RETURN VIOLIN TO IT'S HOME
- CAREFULLY WIPE ROSIN FROM YOUR INSTRUMENT WITH A SOFT ALL COTTON CLOTH
- ONCE A WEEK CAREFULLY WIPE THE STICK OF YOUR BOW TO REMOVE ROSIN BUILD-UP
- BE SURE TO PUT YOUR ROSIN AWAY!

FIND YOUR FEET

LEARN REST POSITION - 1ST POSITION
GETTING READY TO PLAY POSITION-2ND POSITION
PLAYING POSITION-3RD POSITION

FIRST POSITION (REST POSITION):

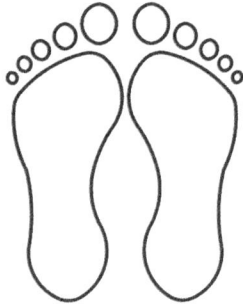

IN 1ST POSITION:

FEET ARE "ZIPPED" TOGETHER

PLACE YOUR VIOLIN UNDER YOUR BOW (RIGHT) ARM

WITH THE BRIDGE FACING OUT

TOES POINT TOWARDS MUSIC STAND, YOUR
BODY FACES THE MUSIC STAND!

SECOND POSITION:

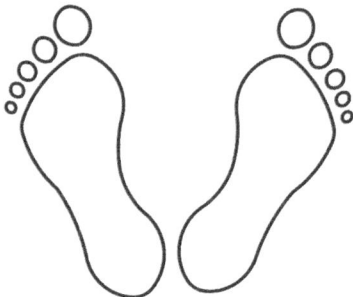

IN 2ND POSITION:

HEELS ARE STILL ARE "ZIPPED" TOGETHER

TOES ARE "UNZIPPED"

PLACE YOUR VIOLIN (LEFT) HAND ON YOUR INSTRUMENT NOW

THIRD POSITION (PLAYING POSITION):

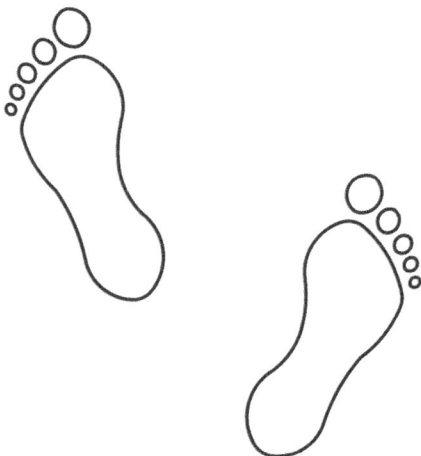

IN 3RD POSITION:

LEAVE YOUR BOW (RIGHT) FOOT IN PLACE

MOVE VIOLIN (LEFT) FOOT FORWARD

TOWARDS THE MUSIC STAND.

PLACE YOUR VIOLIN IN PLAYING POSITION

AND FIND YOUR BOW GRIP

THE REST POSITION SONG

YOU CAN SING THIS TO THE TUNE OF "TWINKLE TWHIKLE LITTLE STAR"
YOUR TEACHER MAY GIVE YOU A SPECIAL MAT TO PLACE YOUR FEET ON AT HOME!

REST POSITION, FEET IN LINE

SCROLL OUT FRONT, THAT'S MIGHTY FINE!

CHECK YOUR BRIDGE 'CAUSE IT SHOULD BE,

PEEKING OUT AT YOU AND ME.

NOW WE STAND-STRAIGHT TO BOW,

HELLO TOES, HELLO NOSE!

You can draw a picture of yourself in rest position or playing position in the space below:

WHY PLAY THE VIOLIN: THE SCIENCE OF MUSIC

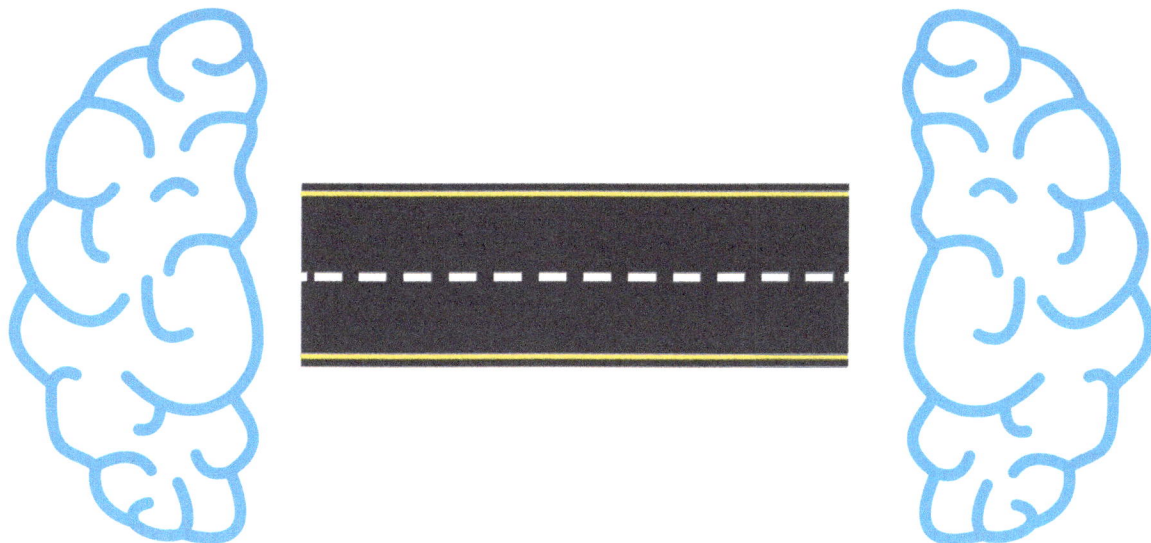

When you learn to play a musical instrument you are learning to use BOTH sides of your brain together at the same time. When you begin there are NO paths (we call these synapses) between the sides of the brain. Each time you practice, it's as if little construction workers are working to make a stronger road between the sides of your brain. You start with tire tracks, then a dirt road. Soon you have some gravel, then pavement, eventually a super highway!
Ways to make your synapses stronger are:
-practicing a few notes 100 times
-memorizing music
-playing review pieces (songs you've already learned)

MORE ON SYNAPSES

Many parents want their children to play a musical instrument. This is because developing strong synapses as a child makes you better at math, reading, spelling-and of course, MUSIC!

Many "grown ups" also want to learn a musical instrument. For older adults it's important to keep learning NEW skills that create new synapses, and no matter your age music is FUN to make!

Did you know?
When you move your right hand, your LEFT side of your brain makes your right hand move?
And when you move your left hand, the RIGHT side of your brain makes your left hand move!

CROSSING THE MIDLINE

When you practice Violin you might notice that other things become easier like:
-tying your shoes
-sports
-cutting with scissors
This is because in Violin, unlike many musical instruments, we "cross the midline." Crossing the midline is when we move our arm or leg across the middle of our body to perform a task. Crossing the midline is vital to the development of babies and toddlers using both sides of the body together, such as putting on shoes and socks, writing and cutting. In older children it promotes the coordination and communication of the left and right hemispheres of the brain. It also encourages bilateral coordination, the process of developing a dominant hand and development of fine-motor skills.

WHY DO YOU WANT TO LEARN VIOLIN?

Do you want to be able to play a special piece of music? Do you like the way the Violin looks or sounds? Do you want to play Violin with other musicians? These are all great reasons to start!

VIOLIN HOLD

WE HOLD OUR VIOLIN IN OUR LEFT HAND. DID YOU KNOW YOUR HEAD IS ABOUT THE WEIGHT OF THE BOWLING BALL YOU WOULD USE WHEN BOWLING? OUR "HEAVY BRAINS" CAN EASILY HOLD THE VIOLIN BY JUST LEANING OUR HEAD OVER. BE SURE YOU ARE ONLY LEANING YOUR HEAD OVER AND NOT SCRUNCHING YOUR LEFT SHOULDER UP TO HOLD THE VIOLIN!

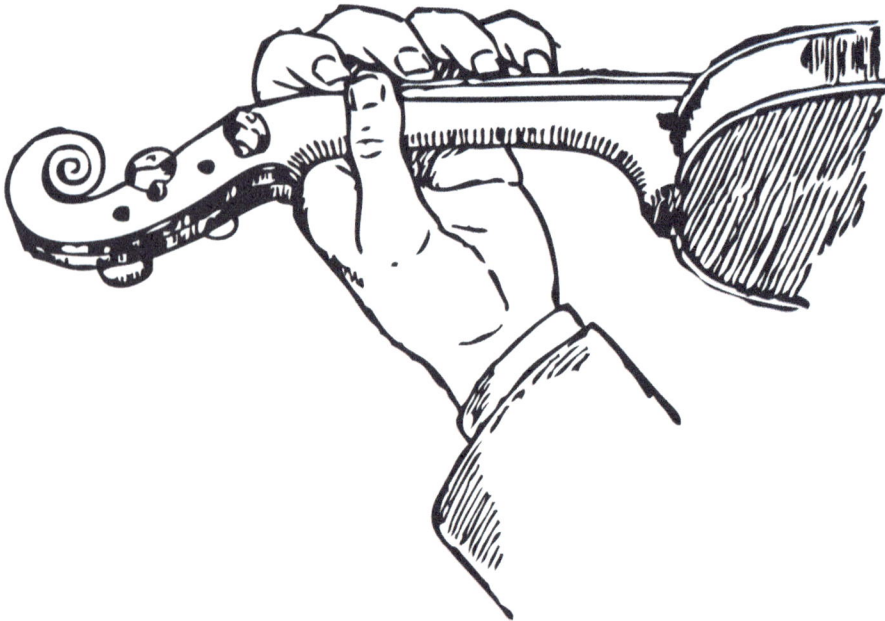

THE THUMB GOES NEAR THE NUT ON THE NECK OF THE VIOLIN.
DON'T HAVE A "JACK-IN-THE-BOX" THUMB! KEEP YOUR THUMB SO LOW THAT
JUST THE TIP IS PEEKING OUT! A GOOD EXERCISE IS TO PUT ALL OF YOUR FINGERS ON
YOUR VIOLIN AND TRY TO KEEP YOUR THUMB IN THE CORRECT POSITION!

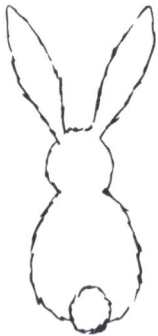

IMAGINE A LITTLE BUNNY HIDING IN HIS BUNNY HOLE,
BUT HE DOESN'T KNOW THAT HIS BUNNY EARS
ARE "PEEKING" OUT AND EVERYONE CAN STILL SEE HIM!
YOUR TEACHER MAY DRAW BUNNY EARS ON YOUR THUMB.

SCAN ME

LET YOUR VIOLIN THUMB BE RELAXED WHEN YOU PLAY THE VIOLIN,
NOT STRAIGHT UP LIKE A THUMBS UP,
NOT BENT LIKE YOU'RE MAKING A FIST,
BUT A LITTLE CURVED LIKE A BIG BANANA.

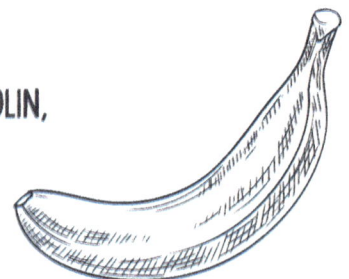

VIOLIN GAMES

USE A BARREL OF MONKEYS GAME TO HOOK ON TO YOUR VIOLIN PEG OR A STRING! THIS ACTIVITY TAKES ABOUT 60 SECONDS AND IF YOU CAN HOLD YOUR FOAM VIOLIN THIS LONG THEN YOU'RE READY FOR A REAL VIOLIN! WE NEED TO BE ABLE TO HOLD THE VIOLIN WITH OUR "HEAVY BRAINS" ONLY, NOT WITH SCRUNCHING UP OUR SHOULDER OR HOLDING OUR VIOLIN WITH OUR HAND.

CAREFULLY PLACE SOME STRAWS IN YOUR F HOLES AND PLACE YOUR BOW ON THE STRINGS ON THE SIDE CLOSER TO THE BRIDGE. NOW YOUR BOW HAS A STRAIGHT PATH TO BOW ON! ON A FOAM VIOLIN YOU CAN USE TWO RUBBER BANDS TO MAKE A STRAIGHT PATH

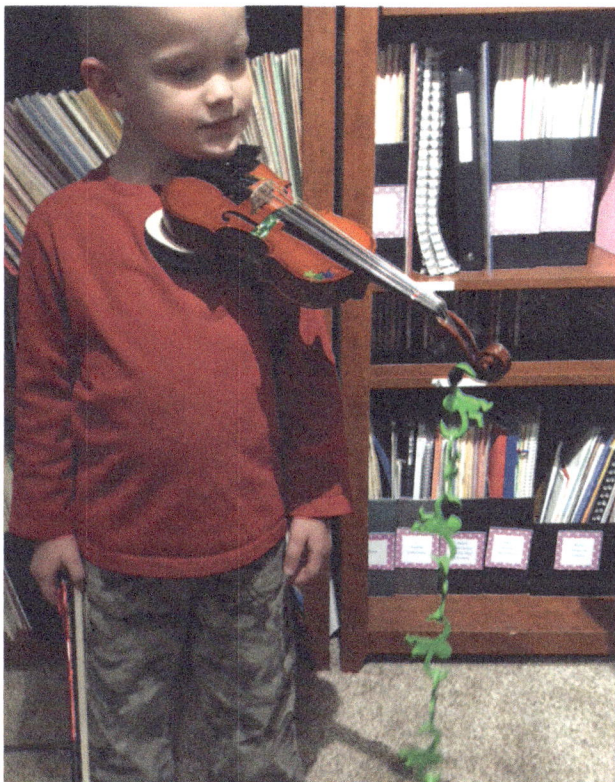

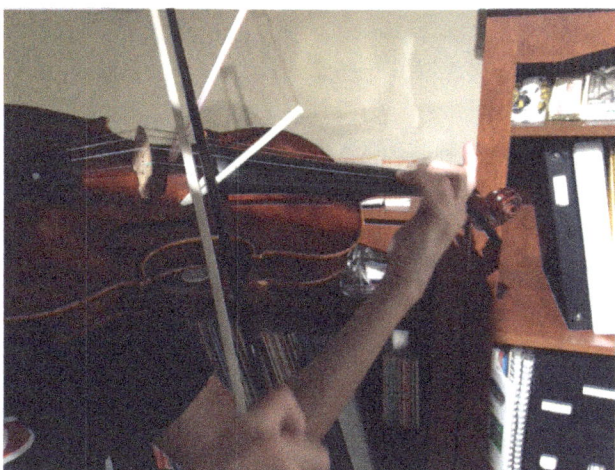

MORE VIOLIN HOLD GAMES:

MARBLE RUN: YOUR PRACTICE HELPER CAN GIVE YOU A PLASTIC MARBLE OR SMALL FOIL COVERED CHOCOLATE BALL AND PLACE IT ON TO YOUR VIOLIN BETWEEN THE G AND D STRINGS NEAR THE BRIDGE. THIS ACTIVITY TAKES ABOUT 60 SECONDS AND WILL HELP YOU KEEP YOUR VIOLIN LEVEL-WE WANT THE VIOLIN SCROLL TO POINT TO THE WALL, NOT THE FLOOR. YOU SHOULD ALWAYS AIM TO CREATE A "CONSTANT" LEVEL PLANE WITH YOUR VIOLIN (HORIZONTAL TO THE GROUND) FOR YOUR BOW TO MOVE ON. YOUR BOW SHOULD BE THE ONLY VARIABLE, MEANING IF YOU KEEP YOUR VIOLIN FLAT YOU'LL BE MORE SUCCESSFUL! YOU CAN ALSO PUT A SMALL SOFT TOY OR CANDY ON YOUR VIOLIN AND SEE IF IT CAN STAY ON TOP WHILE YOU PLAY SOME OPEN STRINGS!

WHICH VIOLINIST LOOKS THE BEST?

BOW HOLD

THE THUMB IS BENT AND WHEN YOU START YOU MAY PLACE IT ON THE SILVER PART OF YOUR FROG.

SOON YOU'LL HOLD YOUR BOW WITH THE THUMB IN THE "HOT TUB" OR THE PART OF THE STICK THAT IS IN BETWEEN THE GRIP AND THE FROG.

YOUR TEACHER MAY GIVE YOU SOME HELPERS ON YOUR BOW WHEN YOU START LIKE A PINKY HOLDER.

THE PINKY SITS ON TOP OF THE STICK ABOVE THE FROG

YOUR POINTER FINGER CAN REST ON THE STICK IN BETWEEN THE KNUCKLES CLOSEST TO YOUR FINGERNAIL.

YOUR MIDDLE FINGERS SHOULD WRAP AROUND THE FROG, MEETING YOUR THUMB TO MAKE A "BOW BUNNY"`

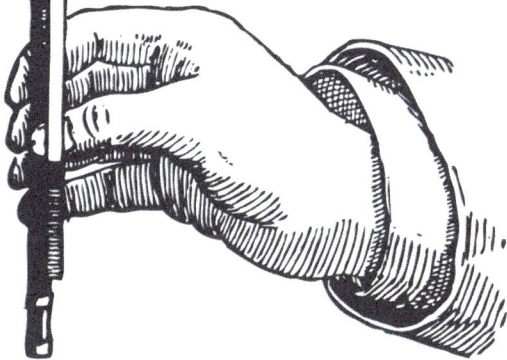

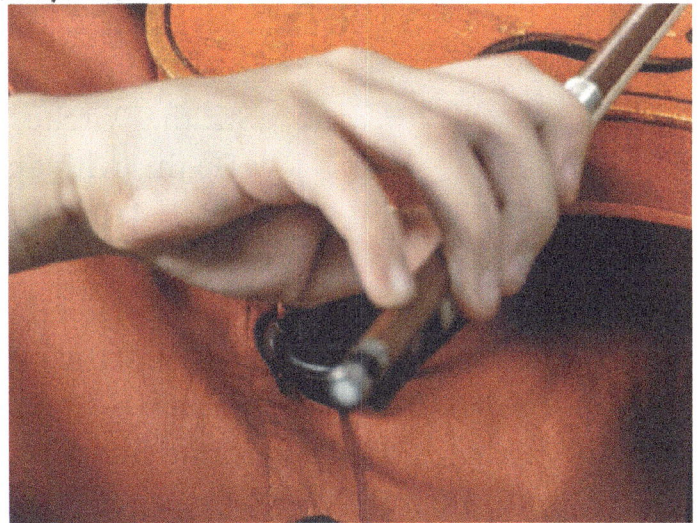

THE HAND SIGN FOR "ROCK AND ROLL" IS A GOOD WAY TO PRACTICE YOUR BOW GRIP. START WITH YOUR THUMB ON THE OUTSIDE LIKE IN THIS PICTURE THEN MOVE IT TO THE INSIDE WITH YOUR FINGERS COVERING YOUR THUMB.

YES, VIOLINISTS CAN ROCK TOO!

BOW EXERCISES

You can practice bow exercises with your bow or a pencil or pen too.

SIMON SAYS

Examples:

Pick up your bow (at the frog, middle or tip)

Build a bow hold with your bow hand on an imaginary bow

Land your bow on your … (head, shoulder, belly button, knee, etc.)

Stretch the bow up to the sky!

Land the screw on the ground

Draw (letters, shapes, fruit sizes, your name, etc.)

Stir some vegetable soup

Shake out your hand

Shake your neighbors bow hand

STIR THE WITCHES` BREW (OR NOODLE SOUP)

Stir the Witches' Brew Stir it Very Well.

Do this with an upside down bow too!

UP LIKE A ROCKET

Up like a rocket (bow moves up toward ceiling)

Down like the rain (down towards ground)

Back and forth like a Choo — Choo — train (side to side in front of belly button)

Round and round like the great big sun (big circle around face)

Land on hand check pinkie check thumb (set on flat palm, look for bent thumb and curved pinkie)

Up like a rocket

Down like the rain

Land on the place where you keep you brain (land screw on top of head)

There are some bow aides you may wish to purchase to help you hold your bow. You can purchase the bow aides pictured by searching "bow buddy" and "pinky hold "at Shar Music and find all the bow hold helper links at www.ViolinJudy.com

LET'S LEARN: QUARTER NOTES & RESTS

QUARTER NOTES-PLAY FOR 1 BEAT

QUARTER RESTS-SHH! BE SILENT FOR 1 BEAT

THIS IS A QUARTER NOTE!

DRAW ONE QUARTER NOTE IN THE BOX:

THIS IS A QUARTER REST! IT LOOKS LIKE A LETTER Z WITH A TAIL. WE STOP OUR BOW

WHEN WE SEE A REST.

DRAW ONE QUARTER REST IN THE BOX:

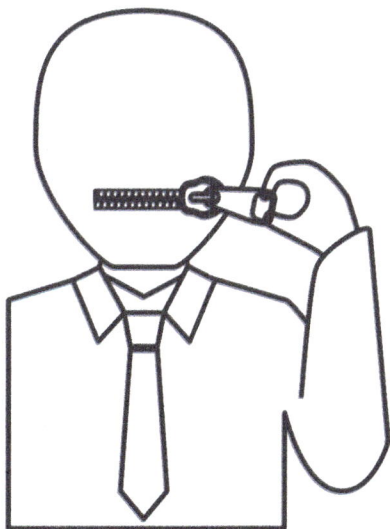

Violin Judy

LET'S LEARN: DYNAMICS

THE WORD "DYNAMICS" REFERS TO THE LOUD AND SOFT SOUNDS IN MUSIC.

LOUD IS NOTATED IN MUSIC WITH-FORTE ABBREVIATION F.

SOFT IS NOTATED IN MUSIC WITH-PIANO ABBREVIATION P.

THIS SIGN MEANS SOFT

MUSICIANS SAY "PIANO" INSTEAD OF SOFT. THE SECRET CODE FOR SOFT IS P.

DRAW ONE FANCY "P" IN THE BOX:

p

THIS SIGN MEANS LOUD

MUSICIANS SAY "FORTE" (FOUR-TAY) INSTEAD OF LOUD.

THE SECRET CODE FOR LOUD IS F.

DRAW ONE FANCY "F" IN THE BOX:

f

Violin Judy

DYNAMICS & SOUNDING POINT

THINK OF DYNAMICS AS CLIMBING A MOUNTAIN, SOFT WHEN YOUR BOW IS NEAR THE FINGERBOARD AND LOUD WHEN IT'S NEAR THE BRIDGE!

THE PLACE WHERE WE SET OUR BOW ON THE VIOLIN STRINGS IS CALLED THE SOUNDING POINT. FOR MOST OF YOUR MUSIC PUT YOUR BOW IN THE MIDDLE TO PLAY MEDIUM-IN BETWEEN SOFT AND LOUD!

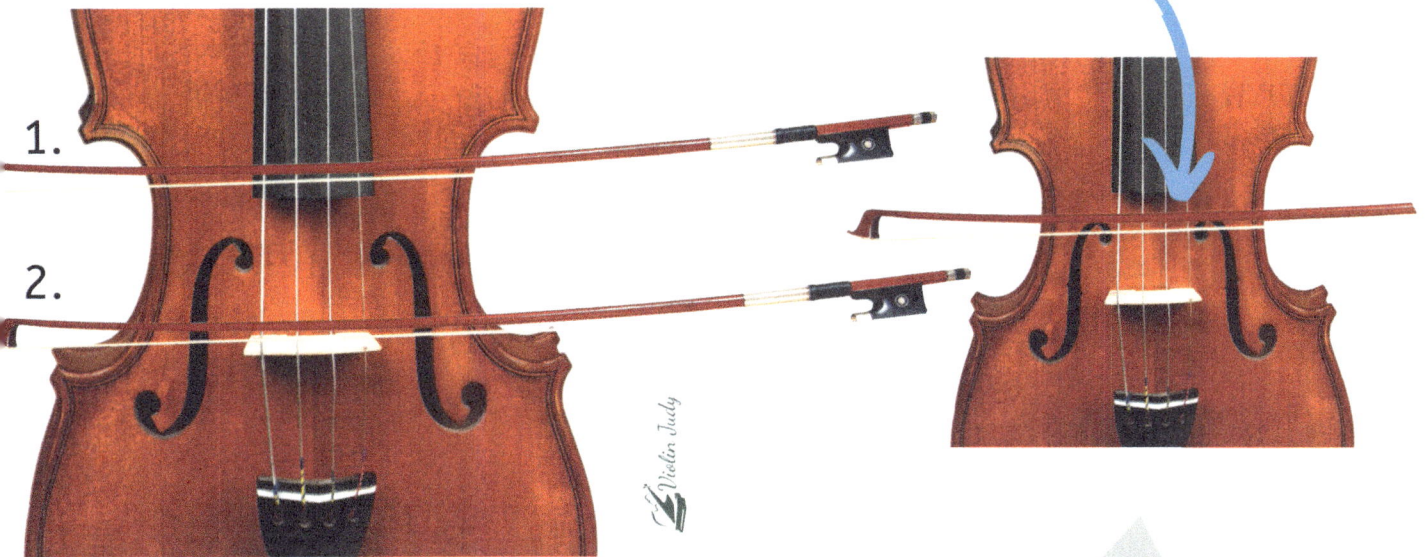

1.

2.

2. Forte - Loud f

1. Piano - Soft p

C. JUDY NAILLON 2020 WWW.VIOLINJUDY.COM

A VIOLIN TWINKLE-BOOKA P. 19

MEAN CATS

REMEMBER TO STOP YOUR BOW ON EACH REST AND ON THE LAST NOTE MOVE YOUR BOW
REALLY FAST AND LOUD AND FLY IT OFF THE STRING! PLAY THIS PIECE SOFTLY LIKE YOU'RE HIDING FROM A MEAN CAT!

SCAN ME

G *string:*

p   Mean   (shh)   Cats   (shh)

Ver-   y   grum-   py

Mean   (shh)   Cats   (shh)

f   Run!

Violin Judy

IF YOU LOVE PIECES ABOUT CATS YOU CAN FIND MORE IN "A VIOLIN CAT" BY #VIOLINJUDY AVAILABLE FROM AMAZON.

DANCING DOLPHINS

ON THE RESTS YOU CAN ALSO SAY THE NAME OF THIS PIECE, THIS SONG IS LIKE A
CHEER FOR BABY E STRING, WE WILL PLAY IT LOUDLY!

E *string:*

f

Dan -   cing   Dol-   phins!

Dan -   cing   Dol-   phins!

Dan -   cing   Dol -   pins!

Splish!   Splash!   Fun!

MY PRO TIP: START AT THE FROG TO PLAY THE FIRST PIECES IN THIS BOOK!

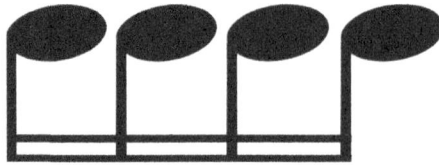

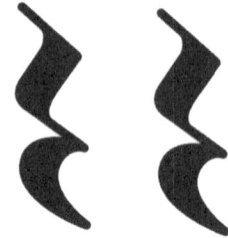

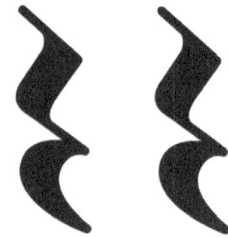

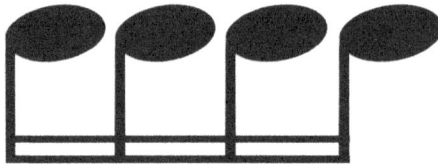

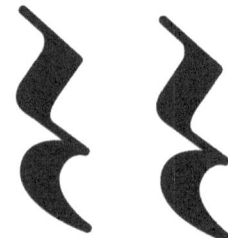

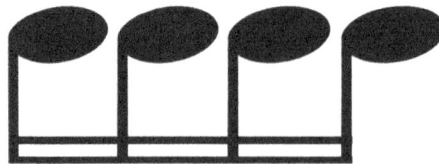

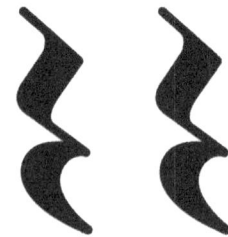

PEANUT BUTTER

TRY SAYING THESE WORDS OUT LOUD WITH YOUR MOUTH WHEN YOU PLAY THE FIRST TIME, WHISPER THE 2ND TIME AND SAY THEM INSIDE YOUR HEAD THE THIRD TIME! DOES THIS PIECE REMIND YOU OF SOMETHING ELSE YOU'VE LEARNED TO PLAY? YOU CAN WHISPER "SANDWICH" ON THE RESTS!

Pea - nut - but - ter

Pea - nut - but - ter

Pea - nut - but - ter

Pea - nut - but - ter

BE SURE TO "FIND YOUR FEET!"
REST POSITION-FEET ARE GLUED TOGETHER.
SECOND POSITION-UNZIP YOUR TOES!
THIRD POSITION-VIOLIN UP! READY TO PLAY!

Violin Judy

JELLY

I LOVE STRAWBERRY JELLY-WHAT'S YOUR FAVORITE? WE WILL USE THE A STRING FOR THESE EXERCISES. A STRING LIVES NEXT TO E STRING WHICH IS THE THINNEST AND HIGHEST SOUNDING STRING. NOTE TO PARENT/PRACTICE PARTNER: THESE ARE EIGHTH NOTES AND THE NOTE STEMS ARE CONNECTED WITH ONE BEAM. WE WILL USE WHOLE BOWS (ALL OF THE BOW) FOR THESE AND WILL PLAY THESE NOTES LEGATO, SMOOTHLY.

Jell-   y

Jell-   y

Jell-   y

BABY ALLIGATORS

THE BABY E STRING IS THE THINNEST STRING ON YOUR VIOLIN AND MAKES THE HIGHEST PITCH .
TO PLAY THESE FAST RUNNING SIXTEENTH NOTES BELOW WE WILL USE THE WORD "ALLIGATOR". YOU CAN USE SMALLER BOWS FOR THESE
NOTES AND THINK "RUNNING RUNNING" OR "ALLIGATOR." NOTE TO PARENT OR PRACTICE HELPER: THESE ARE 16TH NOTES. THESE 16TH
NOTES ARE CONNECTED BY TWO LINES WE CALL "BEAMS." STUDENT WILL LEARN MORE ABOUT THESE NOTES IN A TWINKLE VIOLIN: BOOK B
THESE NOTES WILL BE PLAYED SMOOTHLY-LEGATO.

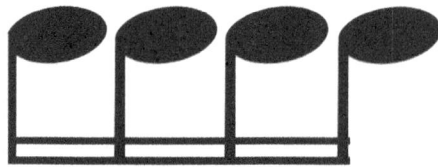

Al-   li-   ga-   tor

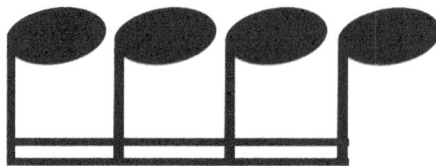

Al-   li-   ga-   tor

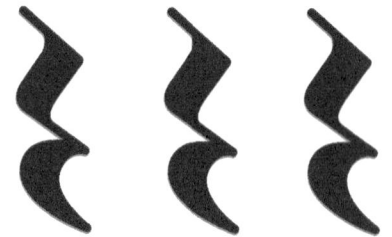

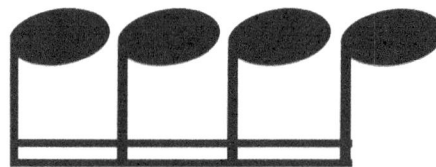

Al-   li-   ga-   tor

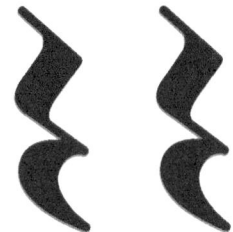

Al-   li-   ga-   tor

Violin Judy

HI FRED!

IN OTHER INSTRUMENTS LIKE PIANO, THERE ARE NOT MANY WAYS TO PLAY SHORT NOTES, HOWEVER IN VIOLIN WE CAN PLAY WITH LOTS OF DIFFERENT STYLES OF SHORT BOWS LIKE STACCATO, SPICATTO, MARCATO, AND RICOCHET! IN THIS EXERCISE WE WILL USE WHOLE BOWS, STOPPING AT THE TIP OF THE BOW TO SAY "HI" TO AN IMAGINARY FRED THAT LIVES THERE. YOU CAN PLACE ANY STICKER OR OBJECT THAT WILL STAY ON YOUR BOW AT THE TIP ON THE SIDE WHERE YOU WILL SEE IT, AND SAY "HI FRED" OUT LOUD, THEN WHISPER, THEN IN YOUR HEAD IN THIS PIECE! ASK A PARENT/PRACTICE HELPER OR TEACHER FOR ASSISTANCE IN ATTACHING YOUR "FRED"!

WE PLAY SHORT NOTES WHEN WE SEE DOTS UNDER OR OVER NOTE HEADS.

GETTING READY TO PLAY MORE NOTES!

IN THIS BOOK WE WILL USE FINGERS 1,2 AND 3

TRY MAKE FINGER GLASSES WITH YOUR HANDS USING EACH FINGER:

MOMMA'S SUITCASE

I GET SO EXCITED WHEN IT'S TIME TO GET OUT MY SUITCASE FOR A TRIP OR VACATION! WE WILL USE THE A STRING FOR THESE EXERCISES. A STRING LIVES NEXT TO E STRING. NOTE TO PARENT/PRACTICE PARTNER: THESE ARE EIGHTH NOTES AND THE NOTE STEMS ARE CONNECTED WITH ONE BEAM. WE WILL USE MORE THAN HALF OF THE BOW (BIG GOAL: WHOLE BOW) FOR THESE AND WILL PLAY THESE NOTES STACCATO OR SHORT.

Suit-   Case

Suit-   Case

Suit-   Case

BE SURE TO "FIND YOUR FEET!"
REST POSITION-FEET ARE GLUED TOGETHER.
SECOND POSITION-UNZIP YOUR TOES!
THIRD POSITION-VIOLIN UP! READY TO PLAY!

THE ABC`S OF PRACTICING:

A: ASK YOUR PRACTICE PARTNER FOR HELP.

B: BOW-IS IT STARTING IN THE CORRECT PLACE?

C: CLEAN YOUR VIOLIN OFF DAILY!

D: DYNAMICS: SHOULD THE PIECE BE PLAYED LOUD OR SOFT?

E: PLAY AN EASY SONG FIRST OR LAST!

F: FINGERS ON THE BOW ARE MAKING A BOW BUNNY!

G: GLUE YOUR EYES TO YOUR MUSIC IF IT`S TRICKY!

H: HELP IS EASY TO FIND-JUST SCAN THE QR CODE ON EACH PAGE WITH YOUR CELL PHONE CAMERA!

I: IMAGINE A STORY WHILE YOU ARE PLAYING.

J: "JELLY" IS AN EASY SONG-PLAY EASIER SONGS EVEN MORE TO BUILD YOUR VIOLIN SKILLS QUICKLY!

K: KEEP TRYING!

L: LISTEN TO RECORDINGS OF PIECES YOU ARE PLAYING NOW OR WANT TO PLAY IN THE FUTURE

M: "MEAN CATS" CAN YOU KEEP YOUR BOW ON G STRING THE ENTIRE TIME?

N: NOTES-NAME EACH NOTE BEFORE YOU START!

O: ORGANIZE-IS YOUR PRACTICE AREA TIDY?

P: PRACTICE VIOLIN ONLY ON DAYS YOU EAT!

Q: QUIET-ASK YOUR FAMILY FOR A QUIET PRACTICE SPACE.

R: REVIEW OLD PIECES YOU ALREADY KNOW.

S: SHARE YOUR MUSIC WITH OTHERS

T: TAP THE RHYTHM OF YOUR PIECES.

U: USE CLUES IN YOUR MUSIC WHEN YOU NEED HELP!

V: VIOLIN IS THE BEST! BE SURE TO NAME YOUR VIOLIN!

W: WRITE REMINDERS IN YOUR MUSIC IF YOU NEED TO.

X: EXTRA FUN AND VIOLIN GAMES ARE COMING IN BOOK B!

Y: YES! PRACTICE WITH A POSITIVE ATTITUDE

Z: ZERO IN AND SET A PRACTICE GOAL EACH WEEK!

KITTENS AND PUPPIES
REMEMBER TO STOP YOUR BOW ON EACH REST.

E *string:*

f

Kit-   tens (shh)   and   Pup- pies (shh)

Meow! (shh)   Woof! (shh)

f

Kit-   tens (shh)   and   Pup- pies (shh)

Now   they're tak- ing   (shh) a   nap!

Be sure to "Find Your Feet!"
Rest Position-Feet are glued together.
Second Position-Unzip your toes!
Third Position-Violin Up! Ready to Play!

LET'S LEARN: DOUBLE BAR LINE ⬣STOP

A DOUBLE BAR LINE IS A SKINNY LINE FOLLOWED BY A THICK LINE. THE DOUBLE BAR LINE IS THE SECRET CODE OF MUSICIANS FOR ALL DONE! WHEN MUSICIANS SEE A DOUBLE BAR LINE WE STOP!

DRAW ONE DOUBLE BAR LINE IN EACH BOX.

Repeat Sign

A REPEAT SIGN IS A SKINNY LINE FOLLOWED BY A THICK LINE. THE REPEAT SIGN IS THE SECRET CODE OF MUSICIANS FOR PLAY IT AGAIN! WHEN MUSICIANS SEE A REPEAT SIGN LINE WE IMMEDIATELY PLAY THE PIECE ONE MORE TIME BEFORE WE STOP!

LET'S LEARN: LEGATO & STACCATO NOTES

A "LEGATO" (LIH-GAH-TOE) NOTE MEANS WE WILL PLAY SMOOTHLY WITH OUR BOW. IF THERE IS NO SPECIAL MARK ON THE NOTE WE WILL ALWAYS PLAY LEGATO, SMOOTHLY. DRAW THREE LEGATO QUARTER NOTES BELOW:

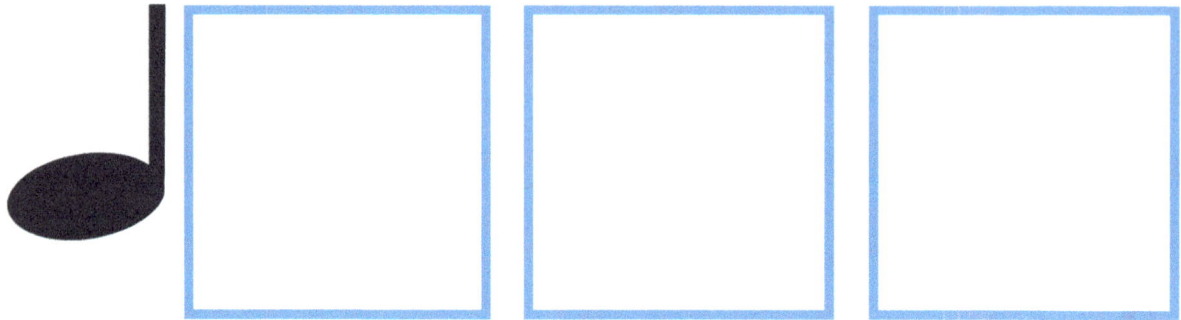

Staccato Notes

A "STACCATO" (STUH-CAW-TOE) IS A NOTE THAT WILL BE PLAYED SHORT OR CLIPPED OFF. THE SPECIAL MARK ON THE NOTE IS A DOT (LIKE FROM THE REPEAT SIGN) OVER OR UNDER THE NOTE HEAD. MUSICIANS HAVE TO BE VERY GOOD AT SEEING WHERE THE DOT LIVES IN MUSIC.

DRAW SIX STACCATO NOTES BELOW. DON'T FORGET THE DOT!

HURRY HOME!

WE WILL USE THE DADDY D AND GRANDPA G STRINGS FOR THESE EXERCISES. G IS THE THICKEST STRING AND D LIVES NEXT DOOR TO IT. NOTE TO PARENT/PRACTICE PARTNER: THESE ARE SIXTEENTH NOTES FOLLOWED BY AN EIGHTH NOTE. WE WILL USE HALF BOW OR LESS FOR THE NOTES WITH TWO "BEAMS" (LINES CONNECTING THE NOTES AT THE TOP" AND A WHOLE BOW FOR THE NOTE WITH ONE BEAM AT THE TOP.

Hur-   ry   Home!

Hur-   ry   Home!

Safe-   and   Sound!

ARE YOU HOLDING YOUR VIOLIN TABLETOP FLAT?

BIRTHDAY CAKE

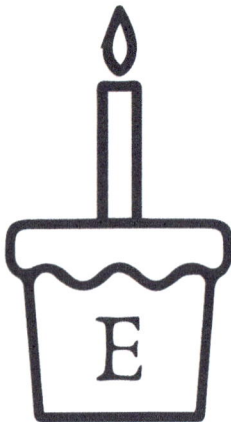

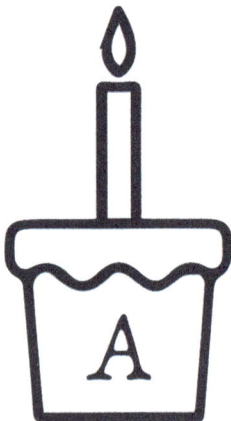

Does this piece seem familiar?

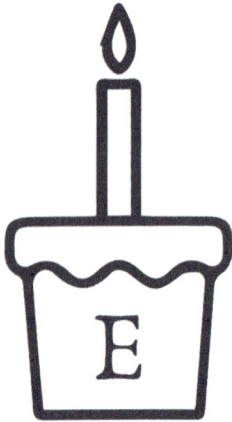

E

Birth-   day   Cake!

E

Birth-   day   Cake!

A

Mom   will   Make!

BABY E AND MOMMA A

THE BABY E STRING IS THE THINNEST STRING ON YOUR VIOLIN AND MAKES THE HIGHEST PITCH.
THE MOMMA A STRING LIVES NEXT DOOR AND HAS A LOWER PITCH. PITCH MEANS SOUND.
WHEN IT'S TIME TO MOVE TO A NEW STRING, DON'T LIFT YOUR BOW, JUST PIVOT TO THE NEW STRING!

Al- li- ga- tor   Suit-Case

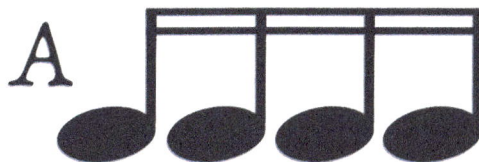

Al- li- ga- tor   Suit-Case

Al- li- ga- tor   Suit-Case

Al- li- ga- tor   Suit-Case

BE SURE TO "FIND YOUR FEET!"
REST POSITION-FEET ARE GLUED TOGETHER.
SECOND POSITION-UNZIP YOUR TOES!
THIRD POSITION-VIOLIN UP! READY TO PLAY!

STRAWBERRY BLUEBERRY RHYTHM

STRAWBERRIES AND BLUEBERRIES ARE MY FAVORITE BERRIES.
FOR THE "STRAW" AND "BLUE" USE MORE BOW AND LESS BOW ON THE "BERRY" NOTES

E

Straw-   berry

E

Blue-   berry

A

Straw-   berry

STRAWBERRY SHORT-CAKE

STRAWBERRY SHORTCAKE IS SO YUMMY! BE SURE TO USE STACCATO BOWS ON THE "SHORT-CAKE" NOTES! AT THE END OF THIS PIECE YOU CAN PRETEND YOUR BOW IS THE CAN OF WHIPPED CREAM AND PUT SOME ON YOUR STRAWBERRY SHORTCAKE!

D

    Straw-   berry   Short - cake   YUM!

D

    Straw-   berry   Short - cake   YUM!

D

    Straw-   berry   Short - cake   Done!

C. JUDY NAILLON 2020 WWW.VIOLINJUDY.COM   A VIOLIN TWINKLE-BOOK A P.35

MOMMA A AND BABY E

This will be easy-this piece looks familiar,
but we need to set our bow on Momma A string first!

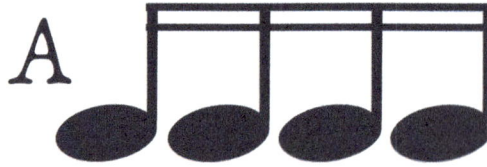

Al- li- ga- tor   Suit-Case

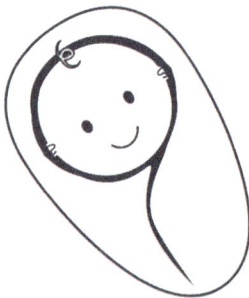

Al- li- ga- tor   Suit-Case

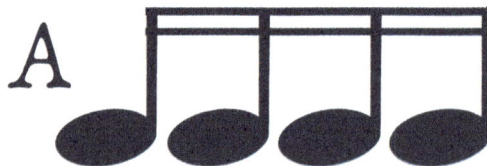

Al- li- ga- tor   Suit-Case

Al- li- ga- tor   Suit-Case

BE SURE TO "FIND YOUR FEET!"
REST POSITION-FEET ARE GLUED TOGETHER.
SECOND POSITION-UNZIP YOUR TOES!
THIRD POSITION-VIOLIN UP! READY TO PLAY!

DIRTY DOGGIE SCRUB SCRUB

LET'S LEARN TWINKLE "RHYTHM A" ON DADDY D STRING!

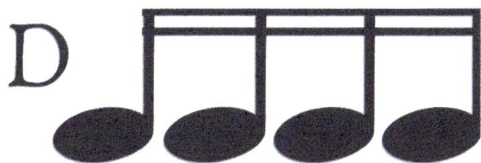

Dir - ty   Dog- gie   scrub scrub

Put him   in   the   tub   tub

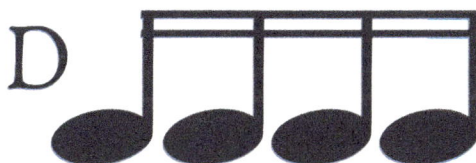

Rub - a - dub - a   dub   dub

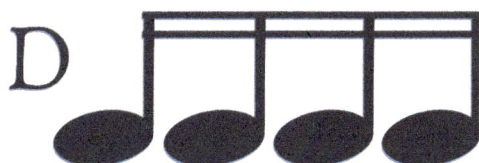

Dir - ty   Dog- gie   scrub scrub

LEARN TO CLAP RHYTHMS!

WE USE MANY RHYTHMS IN VIOLIN MUSIC! ALWAYS CLAP YOUR MUSIC BEFORE YOU PLAY IT FOR THE BEST RESULTS

This is a QUARTER NOTE. Just Clap once! This
note gets 1 beat

This is a HALF NOTE. We say "Hold Me." This
note is empty inside Clap and Slide up HALF
your arm to the "elbow armpit"!
 This note gets 2 quarter beats

This is a DOTTED HALF NOTE. We say "Hold Me Please!"
Think of this note as sad and crying,
the dot after the note as a "tear."
 Clap and Slide up your arm to the "short sleeved" line!
This note gets 3 quarter beats

This is a WHOLE NOTE. We say "Whole Note
Hold It": Clap and Slide up your WHOLE arm!
This note gets 4 quarter beats.

Draw a Quarter Note	Draw a Half Note	Draw a Dotted Half Note	Draw a Whole Note

LEARN TO CLAP RHYTHMS!

WE USE MANY RHYTHMS IN VIOLIN MUSIC! ALWAYS CLAP YOUR MUSIC BEFORE YOU PLAY IT FOR THE BEST RESULTS

This is an EIGHTH NOTE.
When we have more than one eighth note we use beams not flags to write the eighth notes.
TWO eighth notes fit into a quarter and we sometimes say "walking."

This is a SIXTEENTH NOTE.
When we have more than one 16th note we use beams not flags to write the eighth notes.
FOUR 16th notes fit into a quarter and we sometimes say "running."

Draw one 8th note:

Draw two 8th notes

Draw one 16th note:

Draw 4 16th notes

HERE KITTY!

When kitty is outside and needs to come in,
let's practice some cat calling rhythms to begin!
This piece uses a combination of rhythm patterns you have learned in this book.

E — Kit - ty   Kit - ty,   Here,   Kit - ty!

A — Come in - to   the   house   now,   Kit - ty!

E — Hur - ry   home   Hur - ry   home

Violin Judy

A — Safe and   sound   now you're found!

VIOLIN TEACHER TOOL: TALK ABOUT OUR RUNNING 16TH NOTES, WALKING 8TH NOTES AND SLEEPY QUARTER NOTES IN THIS PIECE. HOW MANY WALKING OR RUNNING NOTES FIT INTO OUR SLEEPY QUARTER NOTE?

DOWN CAT UP CAT

HERE ARE TWO CATS NAMED DOWN AND UP. USE ANY OPEN STRING AND SEE IF YOU CAN PLAY
THESE DOWN AND UP BOWS!
FLY OFF THE STRING AND CIRCLE BACK TO THE FROG
WHEN YOU SEE THE ,

REPEAT THE NOTES ON LINES 1-4 ON A DIFFERENT
STRING THEN PLAY THE LAST LINE!

TEETER-TOTTER

Let's learn to teeter totter our bow from A to E with a clean string crossing.
Be sure to CLAP this piece before you play it. Start on a Down Bow at the Frog

Whole Note Hold It

Whole Note Hold It

Whole Note Hold It

Whole Note Hold It

Hold Me

Hold Me

Hold Me

Hold Me

Running   Running

Running   Running

Done!

Look at your bow hand. Is thumb bent and pinky curled?

SEE SAW

THIS PIECE SOUNDS FAMILIAR! LET'S LEARN TO MOVE BETWEEN G AND D STRINGS LIKE A SEE SAW GOING UP AND DOWN FOR EACH NOTE. WE WILL START ON AN UP BOW AT THE TIP FOR THIS PIECE! NOTE TO PRACTICE PARENT OR HELPER: BE SURE TO CLAP THIS PIECE BEFORE YOU PLAY IT.

V

Whole Note Hold It

Whole Note Hold It

Whole Note Hold It

Whole Note Hold It

Hold Me

Hold Me

Hold Me

Hold Me

Running   Running

Running   Running

Done!

G

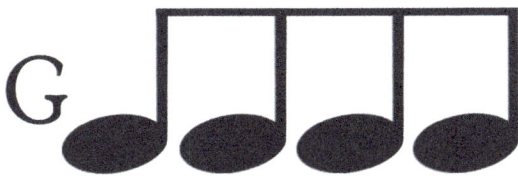

SODA POP

IN THIS PIECE GET READY TO PLAY FINGER 1 ON E STRING!. MAKE SURE YOU`RE HOLDING YOUR VIOLIN WITH YOUR SHOULDER REST.

A

Al- li- ga- tor   Suit-Case

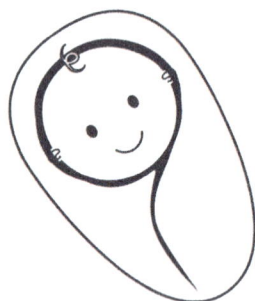

E

Al- li- ga- tor   Suit-Case

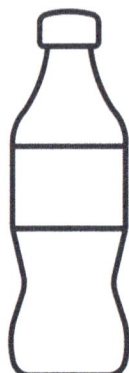

1on

E

Al- li- ga- tor   Suit-Case

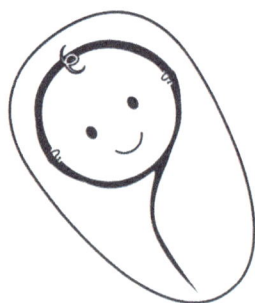

E

Al- li- ga- tor   Suit-Case

STRAWBERRY BLUEBERRY

TRY TO PLAY THESE NOTES WITHOUT STOPPING BETWEEN THE LINES!
BE SURE TO HAVE YOUR 1 FINGER READY TO POUNCE LIKE A TIGER ONTO THE E STRING, THEN POP IT BACK UP
FOR THE OPEN E ON THE LAST LINE!

A

Straw-   berry   Blue -   berry

E

Straw-   berry   Blue -   berry

1 on
E

Straw-   berry   Blue -   berry

E

Straw-   berry   Blue -   berry

BLAST OFF!

PLACE FINGERS 1 2 AND 3 ON A STRING. WHEN YOU SEE THE ROCKET BLAST OFF THAT FINGER INTO OUTER
SPACE (LIFT JUST THAT FINGER UP!)
WHEN YOU ARE DONE WITH THIS PIECE YOU CAN PRETEND YOUR VIOLIN FINGERS ARE
HOT AND BLOW ON THEM!

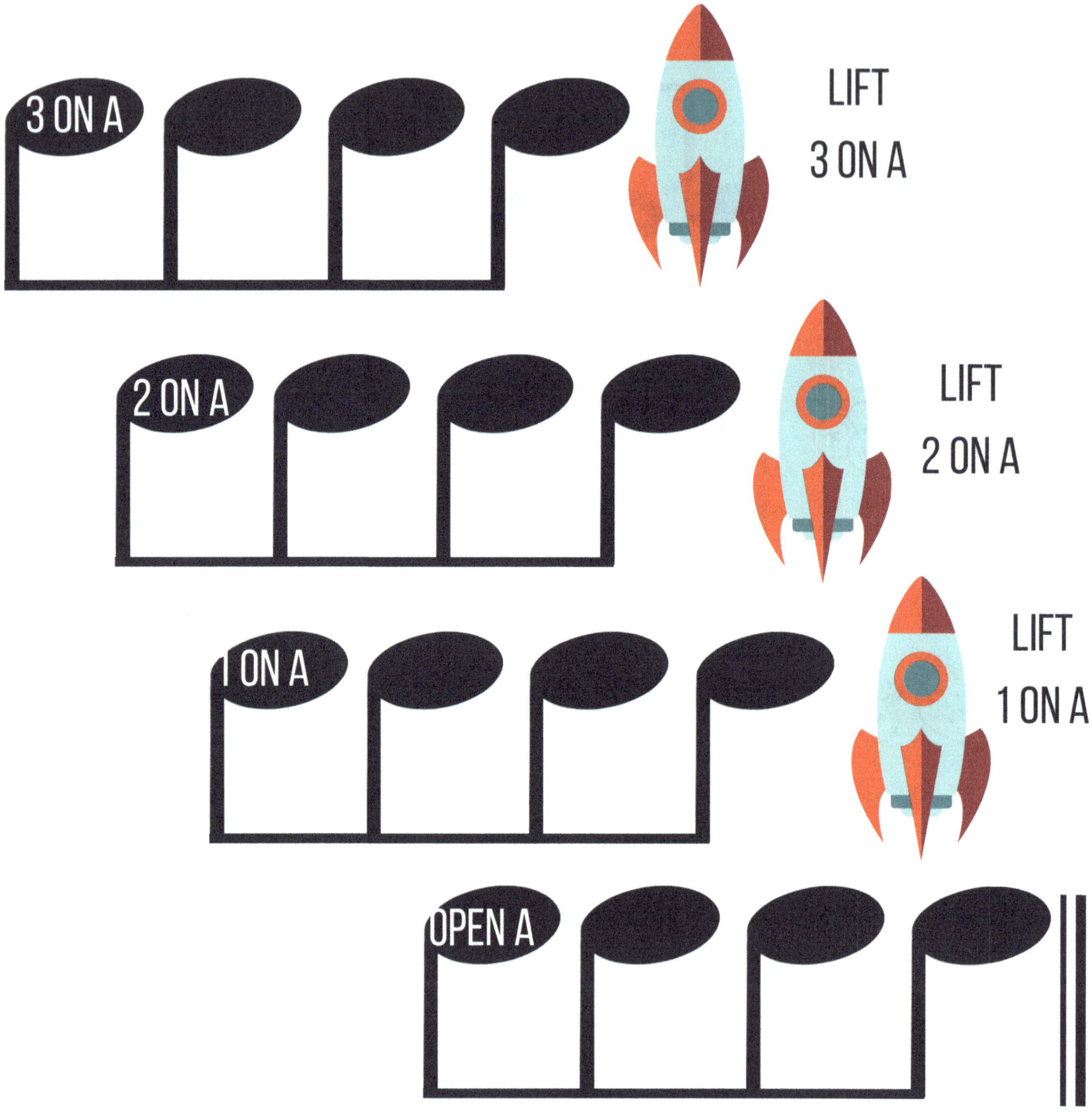

LIFT
3 ON A

LIFT
2 ON A

LIFT
1 ON A

TIGER CLAWS

REMEMBER TO SET 1-2-3 ON A STRING ALL AT THE SAME TIME WITH FINGERS ON THEIR "TIGER CLAW" TIPS WHENEVER YOU SEE THE "TIGER CLAWS."

3

ON A:

LIFT ONLY FINGER 3 TO PLAY

2

ON A:

SCAN ME

LIFT ONLY FINGER 2 TO PLAY

1

ON A:

LIFT ONLY FINGER 1 TO PLAY

A

MATCH THE TERM TO THE SYMBOL!

REPEAT	STACCATO	REST	NOTE

WISH I HAD A 🍉 🍌 💵 🏍️

THIS IS A FUN PIECE! YOU CAN SELECT THE WORDS YOU LIKE BEST FROM THIS LIST: WATERMELON, BIG BANANA, MOTORCYCLE OR MILLION DOLLARS! WRITE YOUR SELECTION IN THE TITLE ABOVE.

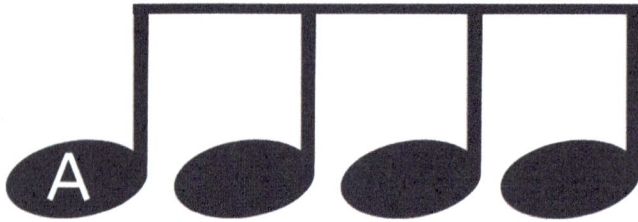
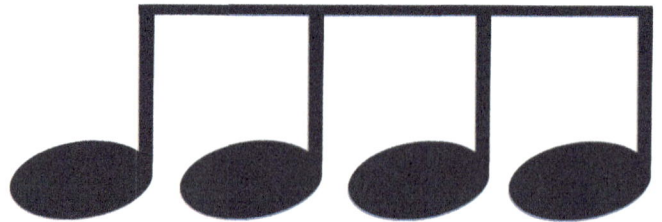

WISH   I   HAD   A   _____

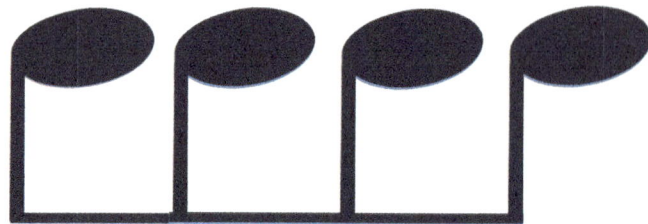

WISH   I   HAD   A   _____

WISH   I   HAD   A   _____

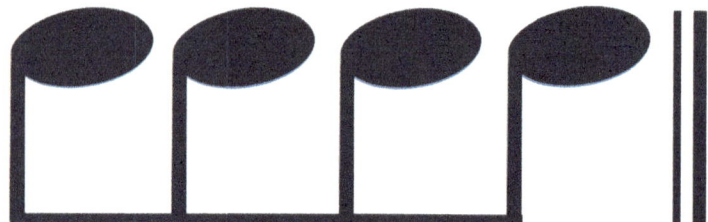

WISH   I   HAD   A   _____

BROCCOLI BROCCOLI

BROCCOLI IS A VEGGIE YOU MAY LOVE OR HATE, BUT ON VIOLIN, IT'S A GREAT WORD TO THINK OF
WHEN WE NEED TO PLAY THREE EVEN, REPEATING NOTES CALLED TRIPLETS.
DO YOU SEE A "SLANTY" (ITALICIZED) NUMBER 3 BELOW THESE NOTES? IT DOESN'T MEAN TO PLAY
FINGER 3-IT MEANS THAT THESE THREE NOTES FIT INTO A QUARTER NOTE AND ARE PLAYED EVENLY!

Bro -   cco -   li   Bro -   cco -   li

Bro -   cco -   li   Bro -   cco -   li

1 on E

Bro -   cco -   li   Bro -   cco -   li

Bro -   cco -   li   Bro -   cco -   li

SHORTCAKE

THIS PIECE HAS ONLY SHORT SHORTCAKE NOTES! BE SURE TO SAY,
WHISPER OR THINK "YUM" ON THE RESTS!

Short - cake   YUM!

Short - cake   YUM!

Short - cake   YUM!

Short - cake   YUM!

Short - cake   YUM!

Short - cake   YUM!

Short - cake   YUM!

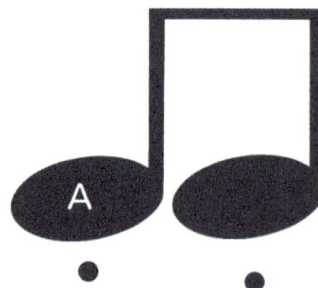

Short - cake   YUM!

C. JUDY NAILLON 2020 WWW.VIOLINJUDY.COM   A VIOLIN TWINKLE-BOOK A P.50

TWO TIGERS

🐾 REMEMBER TO SET 1-2-3 ON A STRING WITH FINGERS ON THEIR "TIGER CLAW" TIPS. 🐾

HOW MANY TIGER CLAWS DO YOU SEE ON THIS PAGE?

E

🐾 3

ON A:

2

ON A:

1

ON A:

E

🐾 3

ON A:

2

ON A:

1

ON A:

WHICH ANIMAL DO YOU THINK WOULD PLAY THE VIOLIN THE BEST CIRCLE YOUR ANSWER!

POPCORN AND ICE CREAM AND

THIS PIECE HAS THREE EIGHTH NOTES PER NOTE! DON'T FORGET THE "AND" OR YOU'LL HAVE
POPCORN FLAVORED ICE CREAM FOR DESSERT-YUCK!

A   A   A
Pop - corn   AND

E   E   E
Ice - cream   AND

1 on E
Pop - corn   AND

E
Ice - cream   AND

A
Pop - corn   AND

E
Ice - cream   AND

1 on E
Pop - corn   AND

Ice - cream   E
AND

ICE CREAM CONE

THIS PIECE HAS THREE EIGHTH NOTES PER NOTE! DON'T FORGET THE "CONE" OR YOU'LL HAVE MESSY DRIPPING ICE CREAM EVERYWHERE!

SCAN ME

3 on A — Ice - cream — Cone — 2 on A — Ice - cream — Cone

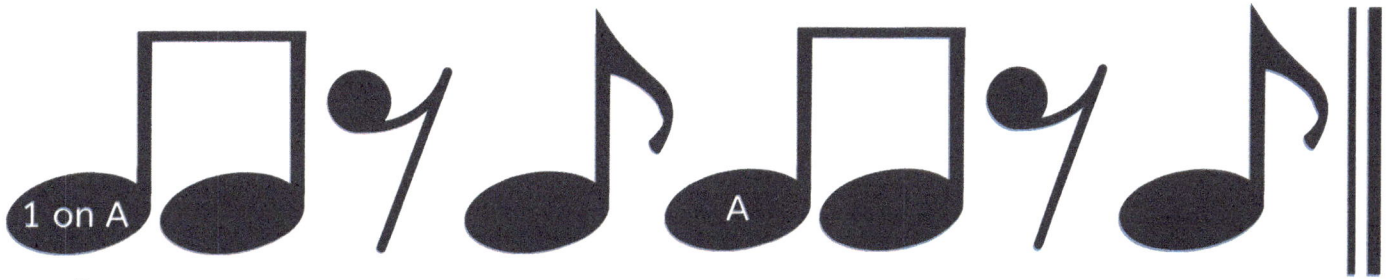

1 on A — Ice - cream — Cone — A — Ice - cream — Cone

3 on A — Ice - cream — Cone — 2 on A — Ice - cream — Cone

1 on A — Ice - cream — Cone — A — Ice - cream — Cone

C. JUDY NAILLON 2020 WWW.VIOLINJUDY.COM

A VIOLIN TWINKLE-BOOK A P.53

TWINKLE COOKIE

- ☐ ALLIGATOR SUITCASE
- ☐ STRAW-BERRY, BLUE-BERRY
- ☐ BROCCOLI BROCCOLI
- ☐ WISH I HAD A ___ ___ ___ ___
- ☐ POP CORN & ICE CREAM & & &
- ☐ TWINKLE ⭐⭐⭐

Violin Judy

LET'S LEARN ABOUT LINES IN MUSIC

WHY DOES EVERYTHING HAVE A WEIRD NAME? IN MUSIC, MANY THINGS YOU WILL SEE ARE LINES SO WE
HAVE TO CALL EACH LINE BY A DIFFERENT NAME OR IT WOULD BE VERY CONFUSING.

THE FIVE LINES AND FOUR SPACES THAT GO IN BETWEEN ARE CALLED THE STAFF. IF YOU SEE EXTRA SMALL LINES
THESE ARE CALLED LEDGER LINES.

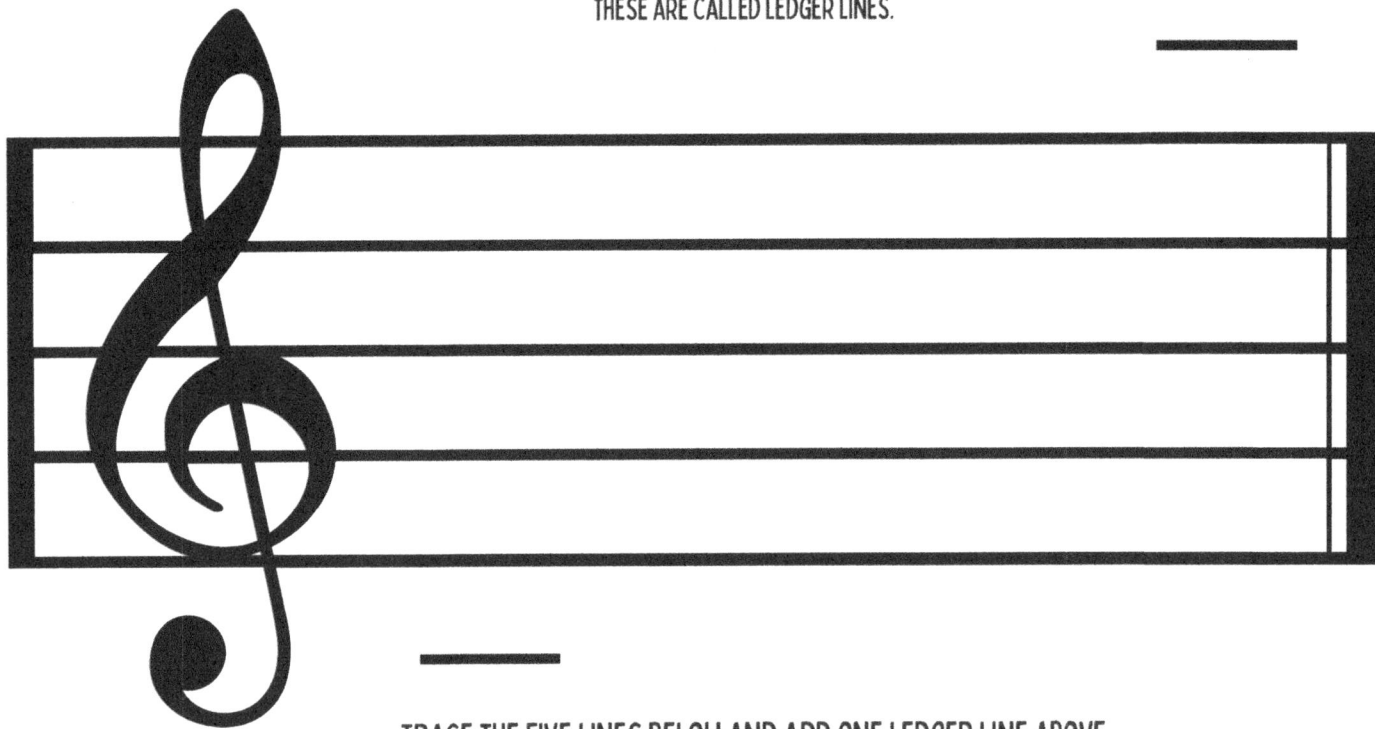

TRACE THE FIVE LINES BELOW AND ADD ONE LEDGER LINE ABOVE
AND ONE BELOW THIS STAFF.

NAMING NOTES-OPEN STRINGS

REMEMBER BABY E LIVES HIGH ON THE STAFF AND GRANDPA G LIVES LOW UNDER TWO LEDGER LINES

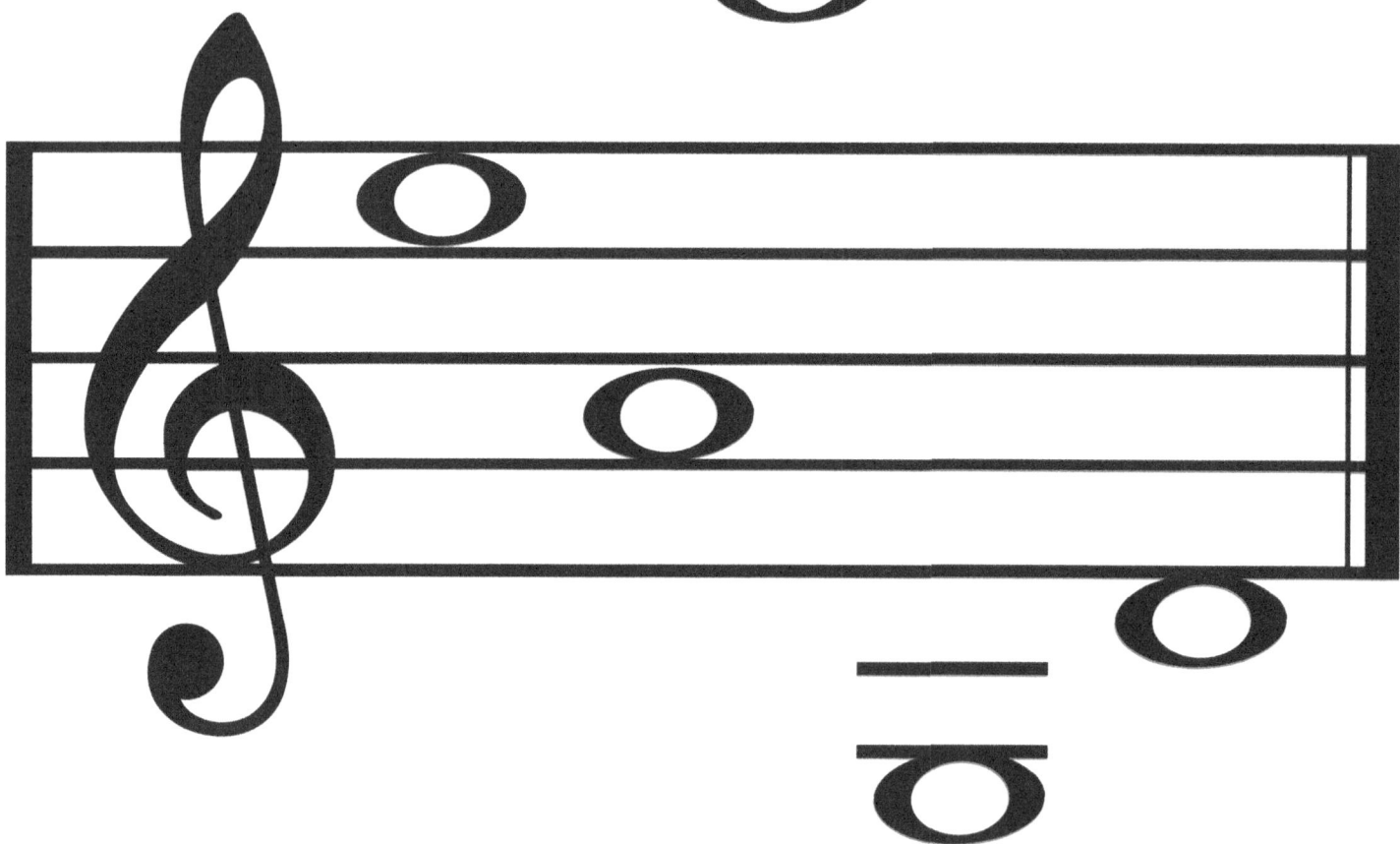

LET'S LEARN TREBLE CLEF

LET'S PRACTICE TRACING THE TREBLE CLEFS ON THE 1ST STAFF THEN DRAW SOME OF YOUR OWN ON THE 2ND STAFF. I LIKE TO THINK OF DRAWING A J, THEN A D THAT HUGS THE TOP LINE OF THE STAFF, THEN FINISH WITH A CURLY 6 THAT CURLS AROUND LINE 2 OF THE STAFF.

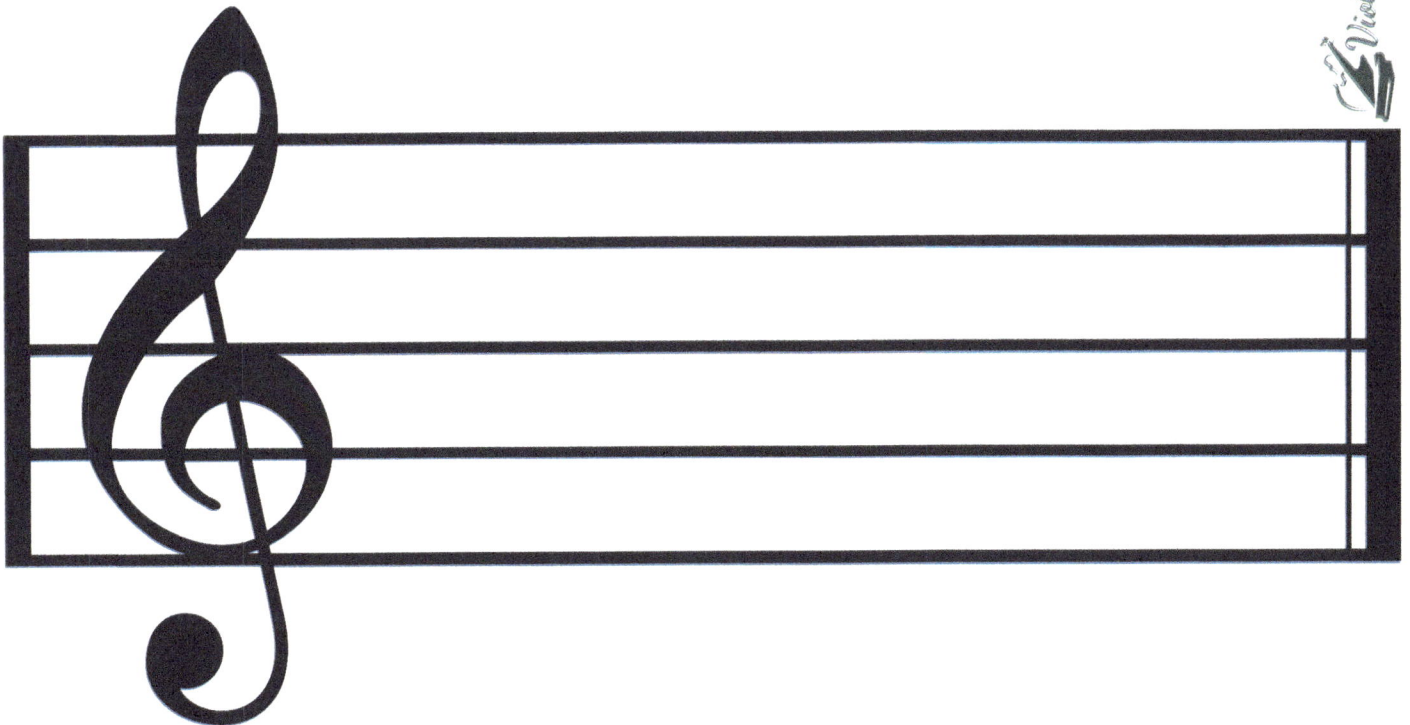

FUN FACT: DID YOU KNOW THAT THE TREBLE CLEF'S NICKNAME IS THE G CLEF?

LET'S LEARN: COUNTING LINES ON TREBLE CLEF

Look at the treble clefs below. We count notes from bottom to top like blocks stacking up from bottom to top. There are five lines and four spaces!

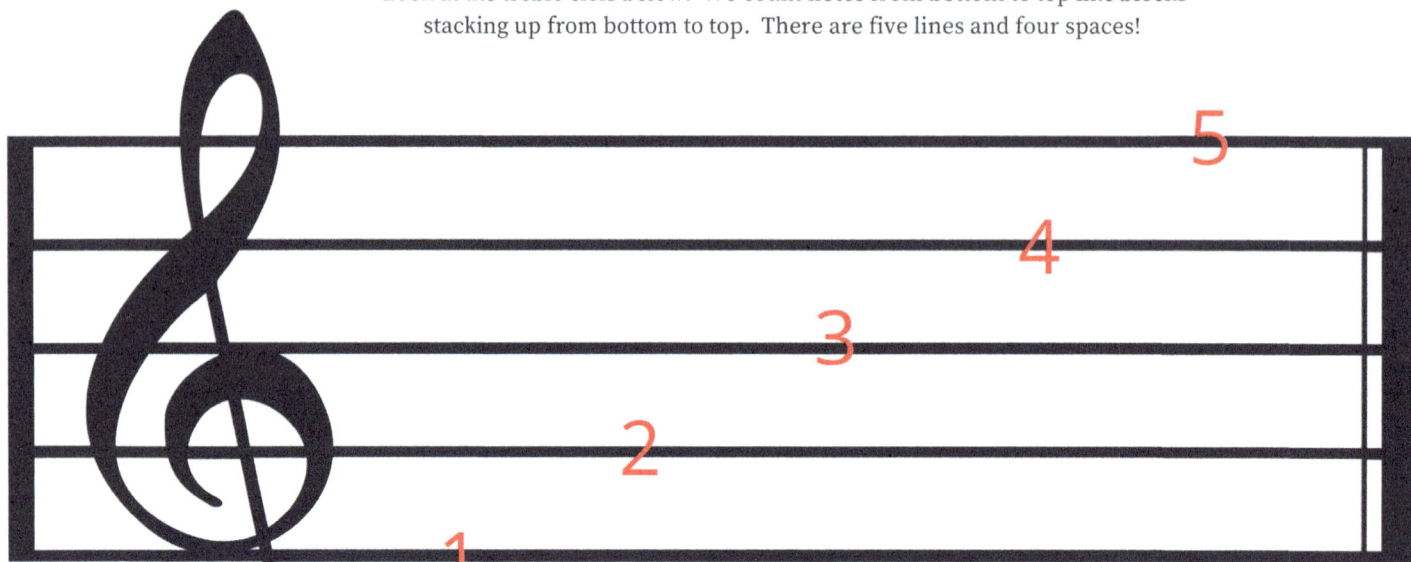

THE TREBLE CLEF'S NICKNAME IS THE G CLEF BECAUSE THIS CLEF CURLS AROUND LINE 2 WHICH IS G!

LET'S LEARN-SPACE NOTES

Label each space note with the space home they live in. Use 1,2,3 or 4.

LET'S LEARN-LINE NOTES

Label each line note with the line they live on. Use 1,2,3, 4 or 5.

LET'S LEARN-SPACE OR LINE NOTES

Write an L beneath the notes that live on a line (Line notes) and write a S
beneath notes that live in between lines-these are Space notes!

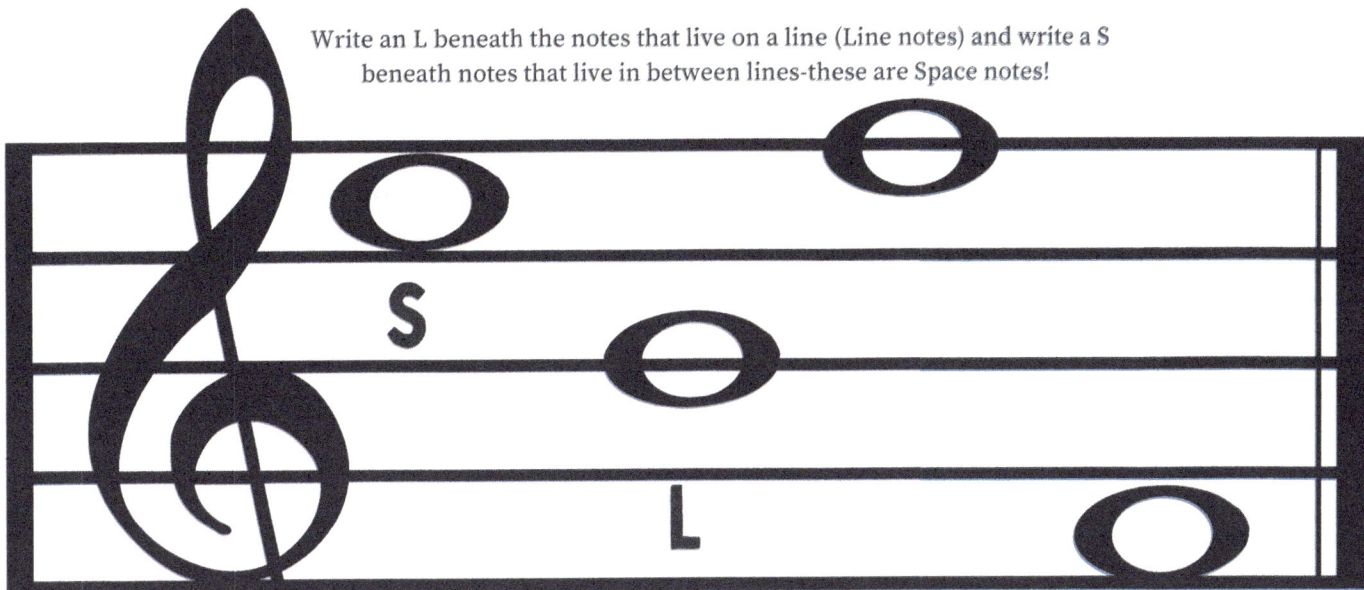

LET'S LEARN- MORE SPACE OR LINE NOTES

WRITE AN L BENEATH THE NOTES THAT LIVE ON A LINE (LINE NOTES) AND WRITE A S
BENEATH NOTES THAT LIVE IN BETWEEN LINES-THESE ARE SPACE NOTES!

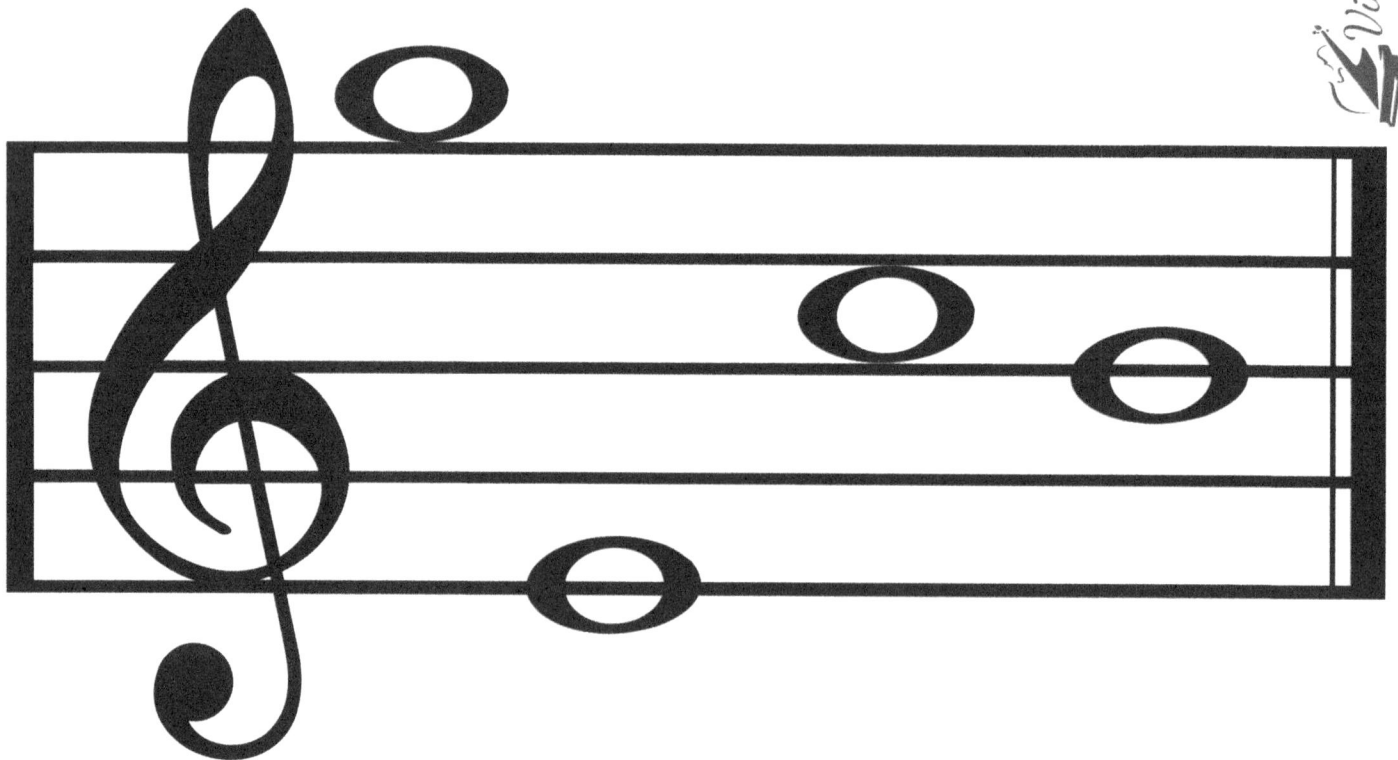

SAME OR DIFFERENT

ARE THESE NOTES THE SAME OR DIFFERENT?
STEMS ON NOTES CAN GROW UP OR DOWN BUT IT'S WHAT IS ON THE INSIDE OF THE NOTE THAT COUNTS. THIS MEANS LOOK AT THE NOTE HEAD !

LABEL EACH NOTE WITH "SAME" OR "DIFFERENT"

EXAMPLES:

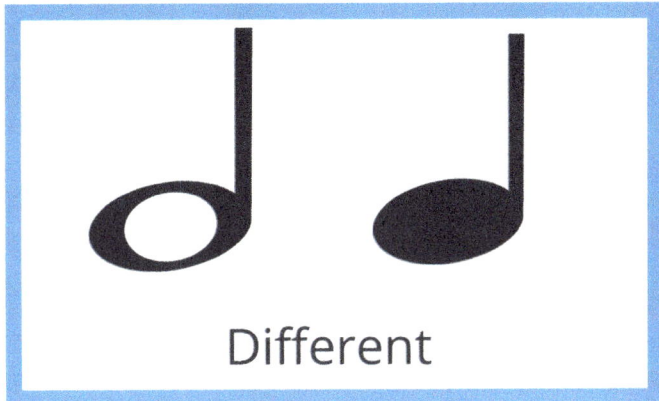

Different

Same

_____

_____

_____

_____

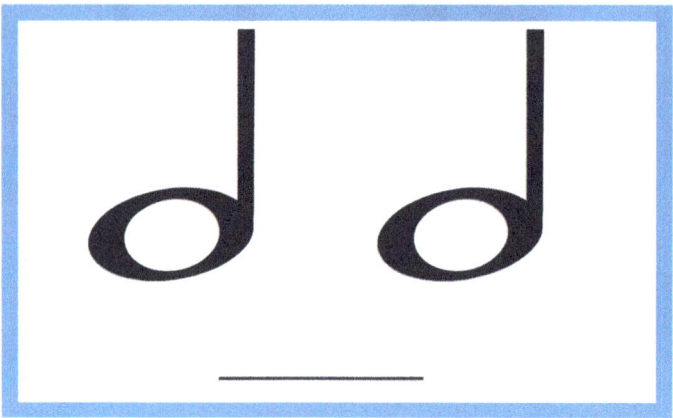

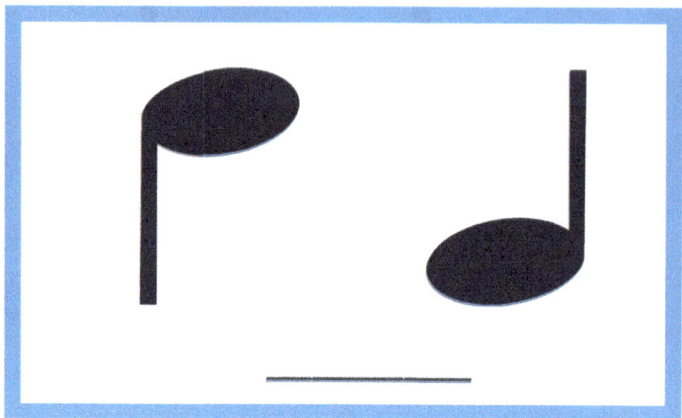

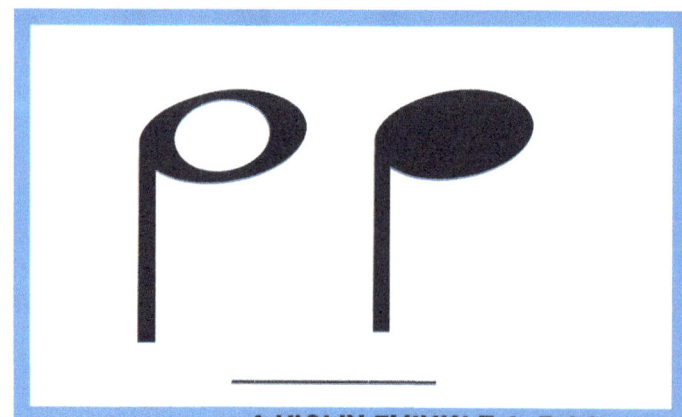

LET'S LEARN-HOW MUCH BOW TO USE?

WHEN YOU BEGIN TO LEARN THE VIOLIN, IT CAN BE CONFUSING TO KNOW HOW MUCH BOW TO USE! YOU CAN ALWAYS LOOK FOR INSTRUCTIONS IN YOUR BOOK, WATCH VIDEOS, OR ASK YOUR VIOLIN TEACHER. USUALLY WE USE THE LEAST AMOUNT OF BOW FOR THE QUICKEST NOTES AND MORE BOW FOR NOTES THAT ARE LONGER IN DURATION.

LABEL EACH NOTE WITH "MORE" OR "LESS" BOW:

EXAMPLE:

MORE   LESS

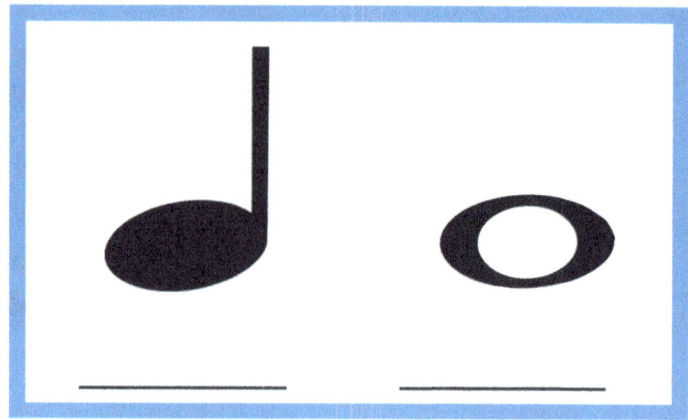

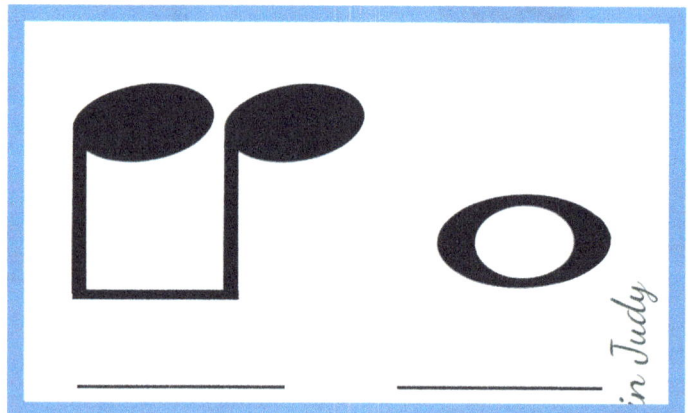

DIRECTIONAL READING

ARE THESE NOTES GOING UP, DOWN OR REPEATING? BE SURE TO LOOK AT THE THE NOTE HEADS!

LABEL EACH NOTE WITH "UP" OR "DOWN" OR "SAME":

EXAMPLE:

SAME

_____

_____

_____

_____

_____

MUSIC ALPHABET
PRACTICE SAYING THE MUSIC ALPHABET FORWARDS AND BACKWARDS!

A B C D E F G

G F E D C B A

FILL IN THE MISSING LETTERS. WATCH OUT! SOME WILL BE BACKWARDS!

A __ C D __ F G

__ B C __ E F G

G F E D __ B __

A B _ _ _ E F G

_ F E D C _ A

A _ _ C D _ F G

_ B C _ _ E F G

G F E D _ _ B _

ALPHABET MAZE

Help the bee find its way home through the music alphabet maze:

ALPHABET MAZE

Help the bee find its way home through the music alphabet maze:

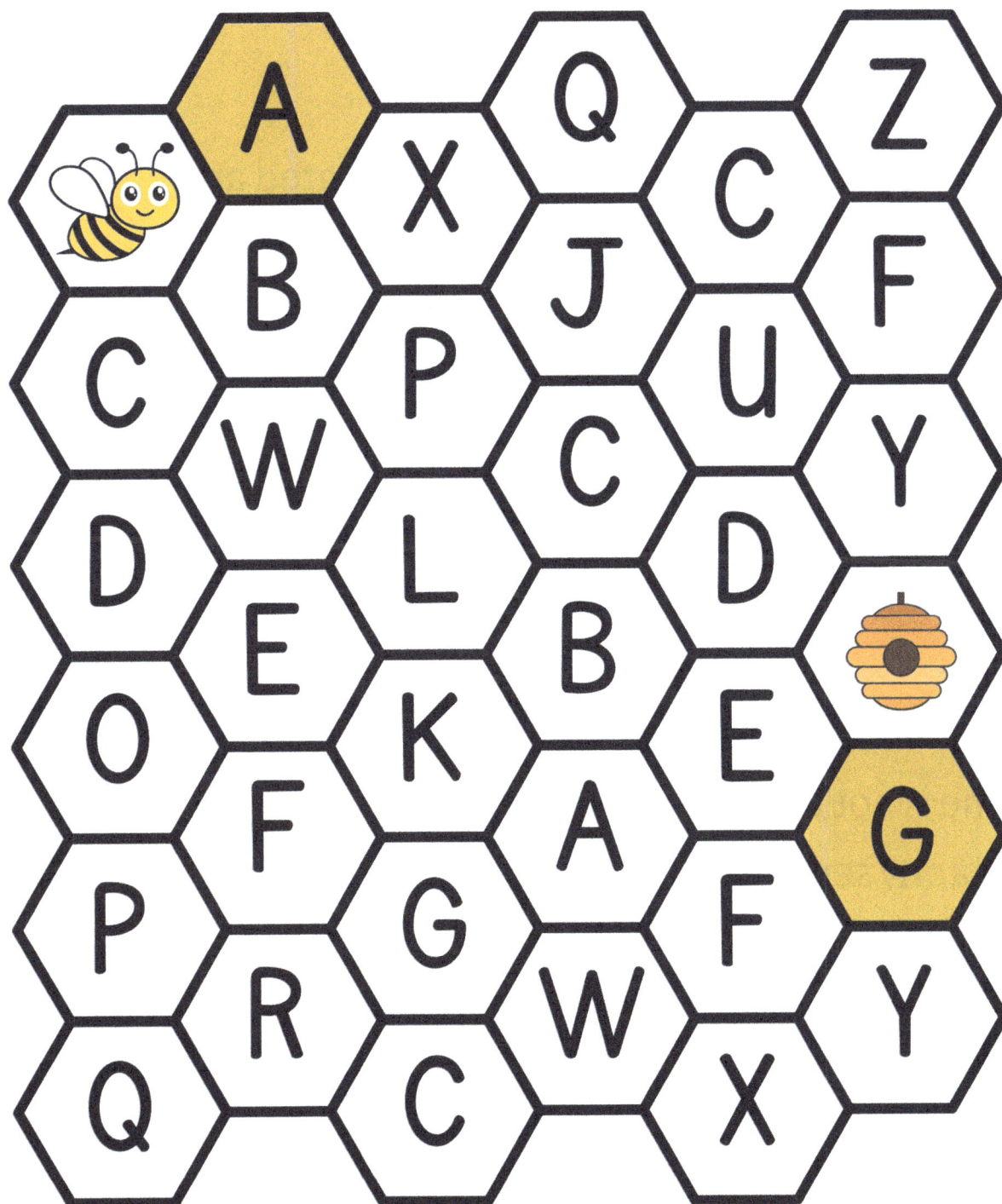

Violin Judy

Mrs. Judy Naillon, "ViolinJudy" is a dedicated and enthusiastic independent piano and violin teacher, composer, author and professional violinist. Her work consists of her large private music studio, as well as playing with her string quartet and Wichita Symphony Orchestra. She served as a church musician for over 20 years and is active in leadership in the musicians' union. She loves coming up with creative ideas to help both students and teachers be successful and blogs about it all at www.ViolinJudy.com and for Alfred's Music Publishers. When she is not writing new books in her Violin or Composer Biography series, she loves spending time with her family and little dog Pom.

You can find more of her books at:
www.ViolinJudy.com

Made in the USA
Las Vegas, NV
24 August 2024